D0375556

A DAY IN THE LIFE OF A
COLLEGE STUDENT LEADER

# A DAY IN THE LIFE

# OF A COLLEGE

# STUDENT LEADER

## Case Studies for Undergraduate Leaders

*Sarah M. Marshall and*
*Anne M. Hornak*

Foreword by Susan Komives

**Sty/us**

STERLING, VIRGINIA

COPYRIGHT © 2008 BY
STYLUS PUBLISHING, LLC.

Published by Stylus Publishing, LLC
22883 Quicksilver Drive
Sterling, Virginia 20166–2102

All rights reserved. No part of this book may be reprinted or
reproduced in any form or by any electronic, mechanical, or
other means, now known or hereafter invented, including
photocopying, recording, and information storage and
retrieval, without permission in writing from the publisher.

**Library of Congress Cataloging-in-Publication Data**
Marshall, Sarah M., 1971-
  A day in the life of a college student leader : case studies
for undergraduate leaders / Sarah M. Marshall and Anne M.
Hornak ; foreword by Susan Komives.—1st ed.
    p. cm.
  Includes bibliographical references and index.
  ISBN 978-1-57922-227-7 (cloth : alk. paper)—
  ISBN 978-1-57922-228-4 (pbk. : alk. paper)
    1. College students—United States—Case studies.
    2. Leadership—United States—Case studies.
    I. Hornak, Anne M., 1972–   II. Title.
LA229.M34   2008
378.1'9—dc22
                                        2007011089

EAN (cloth): 978–1–57922–227–7
EAN (paper): 978–1–57922–228–4

Printed in the United States of America.

All first editions printed on acid-free paper
that meets the American National Standards Institute
Z39–48 Standard.

Bulk Purchases

Quantity discounts are available for use in workshops
and for staff development.
Call 1–800–232–0223

First Edition, 2008

10  9  8  7  6  5  4  3  2  1

# CONTENTS

# ACKNOWLEDGMENTS

We are most thankful to the students and administrators with whom we had the opportunity to work on this important project.

We are blessed to have the love and support of our families. For Anne, her partner, David, has been her rock throughout this process. Her daughter, Olivia, and son, Maxwell, have been a joy in their ever-curious approaches to helping her with her work. For Sarah, her immediate and extended families are to be thanked for their continuous support, encouragement, and unconditional love. Her husband, Dave, and her daughters, Lauren and Anna Grace, continue to bring joy and laughter to her life every day.

We are both grateful to Elizabeth Sabel for her endless editing and compiling of the cases and chapters as we moved through the process. She was always willing to help even when the directions were obscure and ambiguous. We also need to acknowledge the contributions of Natalie Jackson. She assisted with the interviews by transcribing and even largely writing one of the cases included in the collection.

In addition, we wish to thank the graduate students at the University of Toledo and Central Michigan University for their support throughout this process. Their willingness to allow us to use the cases in our classes as well as their willingness to provide honest and constructive feedback was invaluable.

# FOREWORD

## Helping College Students Engage in Leadership

*Susan R. Komives*

" "I am not a leader. I am not the one in charge."

"I am the president of this group, it is my responsibility to make sure we get things done."

"It's our group, we are all responsible for getting things done."

"How can we have so many remarkable leaders in this group, and get nothing done?"

I love it when I meet with a new student group and ask them "What is leadership?" Some brave soul will raise her hand and say something like "Leadership is what the person in charge of the group does," or another student will look at me like it is so obvious and he will say, "Yeah, the leader does leadership." The conventional paradigm we have of leadership is largely centered in our organizational experience that the person in charge of the group (this is, the positional leader) is the only one doing leadership. Further, we have been led to believe that some people have more of the traits or behaviors leaders exhibit so they must be leaders. That may all be true, but it is an incomplete understanding of the complex phenomenon of leadership: leadership is what a person may do from any place in the group and leadership as a group process.

In *Exploring Leadership: For College Students Who Want to Make a Difference*, (Komives, Lucas, & McMahon, 2007) we viewed leadership as " a relational and ethical process of people together attempting to accomplish positive change" (p. 74). The relational leadership model we constructed attempts to show students that when engaging with others in a leadership situation, outcomes will be enhanced when the group is purposeful, inclusive, empowering, ethical, and paying attention to process. Anyone in the group can contribute to the leadership of the group. Further, the goal of groups is to be leader-full and not just leader-led.

Sarah Marshall and Anne Hornak have done a magnificent job exploring diverse contexts in which college students expand their individual leadership capacity and learn and practice engaging in relational leadership with others. These cases are realistic because they were gathered from their interviews with real students engaging in leadership. Recent research on college leadership outcomes found that discussions on sociocultural issues contributes substantially to leadership development (Komives, Dugan, & Segar, 2006). These cases are not easy—they engage complicated ethical issues, difficult intergroup tensions, social oppression, diverse worldviews, and scenarios where outcomes are not clear.

I applaud the authors because these cases include students in positional roles such as resident assistants but also as participants in organizations engaging in the leadership process, such a members of student government. Although many cases are focused on the individual positional leader, students can be challenged to experience the case from other positions in the group (such as a floor resident or chapter member), and many cases do not designate a leader role. From whatever perspective, students can learn that they are doing leadership when they work with others to address shared issues, solve shared problems, and work toward positive change.

In addition to processing cases using student development theories, I encourage readers to use the cases as an opportunity to expose students to leadership theories as well. Educators can incorporate leadership models for college students such as the social change model of leadership development (Higher Education Research Institute, 1996); the relational leadership model (Komives et al., 2007); or other useful models such as servant leadership (Greenleaf, 1977); the leadership challenge (Kouzes & Posner, 2006); or any of the industrial or postindustrial, relational approaches (Rost, 1991). There are a number of useful undergraduate textbooks (Hughes, Ginnett, & Curphy, 2002; Northouse, 2006) that could provide an overview of the social construction of leadership. It is essential that student development educators using these cases gain a grounding in leadership theory to make this an intentional focus of the learning outcomes of these cases. Research shows that helping students learn the language of leadership promotes their ability to differentiate approaches to leadership and to identify their own philosophies of leadership as they develop (Komives, Owen, Longerbeam, Mainella, & Osteen, 2005).

Recent grounded theory research (Komives et al., 2005; Komives, Longerbeam, Owen, Mainella, & Osteen, 2006) on how a leadership identity develops illustrates that college students, probably like most people, hold a leader-centric view of leadership. Living in hierarchical structures we contextualize leadership to be what the leader does (as in some of the quotes at the beginning of this foreword) and we assume that it is the responsibility of the leader to get things done. As one begins to view groups and organizations as entities of interdependent people we begin to see leadership as also nonpositional ("I can be a leader without a title"; "I can be A leader even if I am not THE leader") and as a process ("We do leadership together"). It will be useful to situate these cases in the context that many students may bring to the conversation—that is, a hierarchical view of leadership—and move them toward a broader view of their interdependent responsibilities for leadership from nonpositional roles. Clearly, labeling such roles as leadership will be empowering. Those who do not often see themselves as leaders or who even actively push away the label can begin to see that they are doing leadership even if they did not hold the self-identity as leader.

Most colleges and universities seek to develop students to be leaders in their communities, their professions, and the world. Helping students expand their social identities to include being a leader is an important outcome of the college experience, but it does not happen by accident. The intentional reflection on real world issues evident in these cases will further that goal. But it is essential that students concurrently learn that as much as they can expand their capacity to engage in leadership, it is also a process among the people in a group and organization. Learning how to influence group process from any place in the organization is true empowerment.

## REFERENCES

Greenleaf, R. G. (1977). *Servant leadership: A journey in the nature of legitimate power and greatness.* New York: Paulist.

Higher Education Research Institute [HERI]. (1996). *Collaborative leadership for so-cial change—Guidebook (Version III)*. Los Angeles: UCLA Higher Education Research Institute.

Hughes, R. L., Ginnett, R. C., & Curphy, G. J. (2002). *Leadership: Enhancing the lessons of experience*. Boston, MA: McGraw-Hill.

Komives, S. R., Dugan, J. P., & Segar, T. C. (2006). The multi-institutional study of leadership: Understanding the project. *Concepts & Connections, 15*(1), 5–7.

Komives, S. R., Longerbeam, S., Owen, J. E., Mainella, F. C., & Osteen, L. (2006). A leadership identity development model: Applications from a grounded theory. *Journal of College Student Development, 47,* 401–420.

Komives, S. R., Lucas, N., & McMahon, T. R. (2007). *Exploring leadership: For college students who want to make a difference* (2nd ed.). San Francisco: Jossey-Bass.

Komives, S. R., Owen, J. E., Longerbeam, S., Mainella, F. C., & Osteen, L. (2005). Developing a leadership identity: A grounded theory. *Journal of College Student Development, 46,* 593–611.

Kouzes, J. M., & Posner, B. Z. (2002). *The leadership challenge* (3rd ed.). San Francisco: Jossey-Bass.

Northouse, P. G. (2007). *Leadership: Theory and practice* (4th ed.). Thousand Oaks, CA: Sage.

Rost, J. C. (1991). *Leadership for the twenty-first century*. New York: Praeger.

**Susan R. Komives** is a professor in the Counseling and Personnel Services Department and director of the College Student Personnel Program at the University of Maryland. A senior scholar with the James MacGregor Burns Academy of Leadership, she is co-founder and research editor of the National Clearinghouse for Leadership Programs. She is co-editor of two editions of *Student Services* (Jossey-Bass 1996, 2003), co-author of two editions of *Exploring Leadership: For College Students Who Want to Make a Difference* (Jossey-Bass 1998, 2007) and *Management and Leadership Issues for a New Century* (Jossey-Bass 2000). She is co-editor of *Handbook of Student Leadership Programs* (National Clearinghouse for Leadership Programs 2006). She was a member of the NASPA/ACPA team that wrote *Learning Reconsidered* and *Learning Reconsidered 2* as well as the ensemble that developed the *Social Change Model of Leadership*. She is former president of ACPA: College Student Leadership Educators International.

# TABLE OF CASES

*xiii*

# INTRODUCTION

*A* *Day in the Life of a College Student Leader* is a book of case studies exploring issues faced by undergraduate student leaders on our college campuses. The scenarios in this book relate to student leadership in a variety of key functional areas. These areas are Greek life, student government, residence life, leading minority/underrepresented groups, activities/programming board/fee allocation, service learning organizations/community engagement, orientation/welcome week, honorary/academic/professional association, and general leadership. The cases in each area vary in length to allow for multiple uses. Shorter cases can be role-played and discussed in leadership training workshops, while longer cases can be used as take-home assignments or debated during longer training sessions. Additionally, at the end of the book we offer general advice provided by student leaders.

## NEED FOR THE BOOK

The need to create meaningful learning experiences for students has long been the goal for many faculty and student affairs professionals as they design courses, facilitate undergraduate training programs, and advise student organizations. True learning experiences are situations in which students make meaning of information and learn to process it in their own contexts. Ideally, in these learning situations, students ask themselves, "How does this impact my life and work?" Baxter Magolda (2001) says that "preparing students for life after college requires engaging their minds and their internal selves to work toward the complexity they will need for success" (p. 326). Providing opportunities for students to analyze real-life case studies is an invaluable way to engage both their minds and internal selves. According to Kuh, Kinzie, Schuh, Whitt, and Associates (2005),

> Students learn more when they are intensely involved in their education and have opportunities to think about and apply what they are learning in different settings. Furthermore, when students collaborate with others in solving problems or mastering difficult material, they acquire valuable skills that prepare them to deal with messy, unscripted problems they will encounter daily during and after college. (p. 193)

Case studies provide students with the opportunity to become intensely involved in the material as they work through the issues and problems undergraduate student leaders face on a daily basis. In addition, Baxter Magolda (2001) found that when students are actively and collaboratively working together the opportunities to construct and co-construct knowledge takes on a deeper meaning and has more application to one's own experiences.

Throughout our research, time and time again, students have relayed how little training they received to assume their leadership positions. Most learned by trial and error, others received an out-of-date officer binder, and even fewer gleaned advice from the previous officer. We believe that the meaningful dialogue generated from analyzing the cases in this book can serve as a powerful training tool for student leaders. It is our intent that students learn from the scenarios by role playing and by discussing courses of action so that they will be prepared for actual encounters of these types of situations in their daily lives as student leaders.

## METHODOLOGY AND ORGANIZATION OF THE BOOK

The cases in this collection were written based on interviews with undergraduate student leaders regarding real-life dilemmas and informational interviews with experienced student affairs administrators. These case studies reflect many contemporary and historical issues on our college campuses. The interviews also grounded us in the current roles that undergraduate student leaders play on our campuses. While we realize that our college and university campuses are individual in hierarchy and structure, our goal was to make the case studies broad enough so that they apply across the diversity of higher education. Throughout the process we talked with 110 undergraduate students, in both group settings and one-on-one interviews. We also interviewed 11 student affairs administrators. The interviews were conducted at nine different colleges and universities in three states in the Midwest. The schools varied from large public research institutions to small private institutions to community colleges to midsize comprehensive institutions. Students were contacted through student organization advisors, campus activities directors, and residence life staff. The administrators were contacted by us directly.

We recognize that although some dilemmas on our campuses are isolated to just one area (e.g., Greek life, residence life, orientation), others may impact the campus as a whole. This book attempts to meet both needs. We offer cases that relate directly to a particular leadership role as well as cases that cross multiple leadership areas, for which the issues impact the broader campus community. In addition, we are aware that student affairs nomenclature varies from campus to campus. We have therefore used general terms in describing offices, functional areas, and roles. As you read the cases, adapt the language to relate to your particular campus. For example, in the residence life section, we refer to peer mentors in the halls as resident assistants. On some campuses they are resident advisors, residential mentors, or floor leaders. Another example is that some campuses have orientation, whereas others have welcome week or new-student registration.

Each chapter of the book represents the primary types of student organizations on our campuses. At the end of this chapter and in chapter 2 we discuss how to use the case studies effectively and how to include theories in the analysis of the cases. We also provide an example case analysis from beginning to end to maximize the case-study conversations you may have with your students. Within each chapter of cases you will find a variety of situations all germane to that particular organizational type. Some of the cases can also be translated to other student organizations. For example, some of the details of an ineffective leadership case from the community service section could be changed for use with an underrepresented student organization. We encourage you to adapt the cases to meet the needs of your particular student organization or training workshop.

The cases vary in length. Some intentionally do not offer a lot of detail. We strongly suggest that you encourage students to ad-lib any details needed for them to process the case. As experienced faculty, we have seen many case-study facilitations falter when analyzers hide behind the excuse that they do not have enough information to process the case. If you feel that you do not have enough information, then make it up, add it, or discuss using "what if" statements. Make these statements to fill in details to play out the scenario with different factors.

## HOW TO USE THIS BOOK

While we anticipate that this book will be used by faculty who may be highly experienced at using case studies in their classes, we also recognize that many users may be student affairs professionals who train new student leaders. Our goal is that the book be used as a supplement in graduate training programs as well as training programs for undergraduate student leaders across our campuses. To assist with the facilitation process, we provide discussion questions to begin the analysis of each case. The cases are written broad enough to allow for a variety of possible solutions, depending on the students' vantage point and what they deem to be important issues in the case.

We offer a few suggestions to help you, the facilitator, effectively discuss these cases. First, you should review each case prior to presenting it and identify the questions you want explored by the students. You can use the questions that we present or create your own. Second, you should make any necessary adaptations of the case so that your constituents will understand the terminology and that it relates to your campus. Third, you should understand your campus culture, policies, and procedures, as well as the expectations of your campus leaders, before you jump into the case analysis. It is imperative that you know the rules that govern your campus so that the suggestions or advice you give to students is in compliance with the guidelines of your university. Fourth, if you are unclear about what should be done in a particular case, then you should seek the advice of others before presenting the case to your students. Finally, as a role model for undergraduate student leaders, it is important that you model appropriate behavior for your students. Sometimes doing the right thing is not always the most popular or the easiest. It is essential that you recognize the influence that your behavior has on the impressionable minds of your students. We encourage you to do the right thing and that you challenge your students to do the same.

Next, there are some key steps in analyzing a case. We have found that when using case studies, students often want to jump to what they would do rather than analyze the key points. We suggest that you prevent this premature discussion and use the following steps to facilitate your discussion. To assist you, we pose discussion questions at the end of each case. First, have the students identify the problem or problems in the case. Interestingly, students often interpret each case differently. It is important that you have a clear understanding of what they take away from the case and the central problems that they have identified. Second, discuss the key stakeholders for each case. The identification of key people will help because students can then discuss the possible actions and how each scenario may impact each constituent. Third, identify possible courses of action and how each action might play out. This is a critical step in case analysis. Again, many students will opt for a quick solution without properly weighing out each possible course of action and its potential impact. As you play out each proposed course of action, challenge the students to think about the pros and cons of each idea. What is the potential long- or short-term impact? They should also consider campus policies and procedures, legal constraints, and reactions from various stakeholders. Once they have thoroughly weighed each possible action and its potential consequences, have them select the best scenario.

As mentioned earlier, these cases can be used in a variety of ways. They can be used as written assignments by having students take the cases home and prepare written responses. They also can be read to the students and then discussed. These discussions can take place in larger group settings or in smaller break-out groups. They can also be discussed one-on-one between a student and his or her advisor. We suggest that student organization advisors not only use these cases at the beginning of the year to train new student leaders but also consider reading one case at the beginning of each meeting and then discuss it as a group. This would be a meaningful way to continue students' leadership training throughout the school year.

Another way to use these case studies is to role-play the scenarios. One technique is to ask for volunteers or assign roles from the case to the students. The case is read and then the students are asked to play out the scenario. They are given permission to be creative and let the role play evolve. A couple of minutes into the role play, other students are allowed to participate by "tapping out" one of the key participants in the role play. For example, in a case involving a student leader and an advisor, you, as the facilitator, would assign each role to students who, in turn, would start to play out the scenario. After a given amount of time, you would give a signal that they may be tapped out by someone observing the role play. In other words, a member from the audience would approach the scenario while it is in progress, tap one of the actors on the shoulder, and take his or her place in the role play. The original person would then take a seat in the audience and the new person would pick up the role play where the former player left off. This is an excellent way to let others be involved and can also exemplify how others approach situations differently. Speaking from experience, we have found that students enjoy this activity and appreciate that they can tap into a scenario if they are frustrated with how it is progressing or save someone who is floundering and does not know how to respond given the dilemma.

In conclusion, we encourage you to use this book regularly and enjoy the many discussions that will ensue from reading the cases. Although exploring cases will never fully prepare student leaders for what they will encounter in real life, it is an excellent way to help students determine what they should do and how they should do it. It is our hope that discussions surrounding these cases will help train future leaders, allow for critical analysis, and inspire meaningful reflection. These cases can be powerful tools to challenge our students and their decision making. Use them to aid our students in developing their leadership abilities and to create deep and worthwhile learning experiences.

# 2

# THE APPLICATION OF
# STUDENT DEVELOPMENT
# THEORY IN CASE ANALYSIS

S tudent development theories serve an important role in the explanation and prediction of student behavior. Theories serve as tools in our
analysis of student behavior and program development. College students navigate the college terrain academically, socially, morally, and even
physically as they negotiate their identities and ask life questions such as,
Who am I? and Who do I want to be? The theories associated with college
students and their development give us the scaffolding to explain these behaviors as we train leaders and develop programs to facilitate their success.

This chapter discusses the use of student development theory to analyze
students' responses to the cases in this book. At the end of the chapter, we
cite texts in the literature that discuss other theories that can be used for
analysis. There are many theories that can provide a better understanding of
situations than other theories can. However, it is more important to provide
the opportunity for students to think about analysis through a theoretical
lens, rather than get stuck on the best theory for each situation. As students
develop more sophisticated ways of analyzing and making sense of situations,
you can focus more on that aspect of development.

In this chapter, we take a case study from the book and analyze it without using theory during the discussion. Then we take the same case and analyze it through a theoretical lens. The issues are the same, but the discussion
changes as you begin to focus more on the developmental issues of your students. It is our hope that as you use this book in your own training programs
and courses, you will use the developmental theories in the analysis of the
cases, as well as a lens through which to understand the development of the

students who are processing the case. It is your role as the facilitator to introduce and guide the discussion using a theoretical lens. In addition to student development theory, it is also important to understand and appreciate the influence of college and university environments, student characteristics, the types of experiences that students encounter while in college, and how they process and react to those experiences. Your students (especially undergraduate student leaders) are not going to have knowledge of or experience in accurately applying these ideas. These are tools for you to use in making sense of how students interpret and respond to the cases.

The following analysis looks at a student organization case. The discussion that you have with your students may be different depending on the issues that they choose, their position in the organization, and the demographics of the institution. In the second analysis, the theories that you use to guide the discussion may vary depending on the development aspects of your students.

## Same Old, Same Old: Analysis Without the Use of Theory

Your organization consists of freshmen through seniors. Your organization likes tradition. You have a tendency to plan the same events year after year, because they are successful and popular, especially among your new members. For example, every year you have a toga party, which is always very popular. Each year the new freshmen and sophomores insist that you keep this theme because they want to experience the toga party. However, the juniors and seniors are bored with this theme, and this year the seniors insist that you change it. They have had to put up with the same theme for three years and want something new. They will not support the toga party and will plan their own event if the organization opts not to change it.

**What are the issues in this case?**
They are as follows:

- The newer members want to experience traditional events that are part of the culture and history of the organization.
- The newer members see these events as being successful and popular and do not see a reason to change.

- The newer members do not understand how the junior and senior members could be bored with events that are fun and popular.
- The junior and senior members would like to see new and different events added to the schedule.
- The junior and senior members are bored and have an attitude of "Been there, done that."
- The seniors plan to host a different theme party and potentially pull away from the toga party if the freshmen and sophomores insist on the event.
- The power struggle and infighting in the organization suggest that the group may have difficulty maintaining unity.

**If you are the leader of this student organization, what are your options for handling the issues? Which option do you prefer?**

One preferred option of this organization would be to hold a vote of the organization's full membership. It is important to empower groups and make everyone feel like contributing members of the organization. This option would also break down some of the power issues within the organization and take away the age hierarchy that this group clearly possesses. The students involved with this organization are testing their roles within the group.

As the leader of this organization, consider taking the following steps:

1. Assess who is taking what stand and how those individuals are presenting their opinions (it is important to assess whether this is a power struggle with the seniors versus the younger members).
2. Discuss with the leadership team the issues involved with this situation and find out how this group feels.
3. Talk with all members of the group (as a group) and find out how the group feels about the party ideas.
4. Ask the group for three solutions that can be explored, including different party themes.
5. Present the party themes and the possibility of combining themes; for example, a toga/favorite movie theme party. Get creative with the members of the group and have them think outside the box.
6. Take a vote on the party theme using the three presented and possibly even the combined themes.

We suggest a vote of the entire membership because it is important to take into account age and perceived status within the organization's leadership. It is common that seniors hold most of the high-level leadership positions in organizations, with juniors being second. If only the officers of the organization decide, then obviously the juniors and seniors would have an advantage. The idea of voting would encourage involvement by all leadership team members, instead of highlighting power within the group. It is important to empower all levels of leadership, especially because the younger students will be the organization's future leaders.

**Do our organizations ever get so entrenched in tradition that we lose creativity?**

Our organizations do get extremely entrenched in tradition, and losing creativity is always a risk. Many student organizations are so steeped in traditions that having events that are different seems to take away from tradition rather than lead to newer and better traditions. This is common, because most colleges and universities are steeped in tradition. Magolda (2001) says that "formal campus rituals . . . respond to a basic human need to be part of a larger and distinct social entity (community)" (p. 3). Student organizations fill this need for our students, and when students hear stories about past events, they have a desire to be part of those events. On the other hand, the seniors' boredom is another issue in this case. Because the older students are more developmentally advanced, they are less likely to favor the status quo. On the contrary, they will challenge the existing traditions by focusing on their needs versus the needs of the greater organization. Organizational advisors and leaders need to think about ways to balance being creative and holding on to the traditions that the membership holds dear.

**Do you talk about the varying needs of your constituents? How does your organization meet the needs of all its members? Do you create goals for your organization and challenge each other to come up with something new that meets the needs of your various members?**

Discussing as a group the varying needs of all members is an important aspect of this case. It is important as leaders to make sure everyone has a voice. Hearing from everyone creates a great opportunity for the group to look across annual programming and allows for the emergence of new ideas. Often better solutions can develop from the discourse generated by multiple opinions. Challenging your group to set and prioritize annual goals is one way to review the mission and purpose of your organization, along with your programming. It also allows the group to grow and expand beyond the previous year's efforts. We encourage the organization to respect current traditions but also to look beyond what you have always done and consider the possibilities surrounding what you could do. To maximize the potential of your organization, it is imperative that the group be open to and respect ideas from all its members.

## Same Old, Same Old: Analysis With the Use of Theory

Your organization consists of freshmen through seniors. Your organization likes tradition. You have a tendency to plan the same events year after year, because they are successful and popular, especially among your new members. For example, every year you have a toga party, which is always very popular. Each year the new freshmen and sophomores insist that you keep this theme because they want to experience the toga party. However, the juniors and seniors are bored with this theme, and this year the seniors insist that you change it. They have had to put up with the same theme for three years and want something new. They will not support the toga party and will plan their own event if the organization opts not to change it.

**What are the issues in this case?**
The issues in this case remain the same and are again listed:

- The newer members want to experience traditional events that are part of the culture and history of the organization.
- The newer members see these events as being successful and popular and do not see a reason to change.
- The newer members do not understand how the junior and senior members could be bored with events that are fun and popular.
- The junior and senior members would like to see new and different events added to the schedule.
- The junior and senior members are bored and have an attitude of "Been there, done that."
- The seniors plan to host a different theme party and potentially pull away from the toga party if the freshmen and sophomores insist on the event.
- The power struggle and infighting in the organization suggest that the group may have difficulty maintaining unity.

**If you are the leader of this student organization, what are your options for handling the issues? Which option do you prefer?**

As the leader of this organization, consider doing the following:

1.  Assess who is taking what stand and how those individuals are presenting their opinions (it is important to assess whether this is a power struggle with the seniors versus the younger members).
2.  Discuss with the leadership team the issues involved with this situation and find out how this group feels.
3.  Talk with all members of the group (as a group) and find out how the group feels about the party ideas.
4.  Ask the group for three solutions that can be explored, including different party themes.
5.  Present the party themes and the possibility of combining themes; for example, a toga/favorite movie theme party. Get creative with the members of the group and have them think outside the box.
6.  Take a vote on the party theme using the three presented and possibly even the combined themes.

There are multiple theories that address students' behavior at various points in their journey through college. As a leader of the organization, you could work through the analysis by using Astin's Theory of Involvement (1984) and discussing how meaningful involvement in a student organization impacts connectedness and personal development. The theory discusses the levels of involvement and engagement. It is important that as the facilitator you highlight that student growth and learning are taking place at a higher level with active involvement. Therefore, according to Astin's theory you would not want to create a situation in which some students do not feel as connected and thus lose interest; rather, you would want to find a balance so that all students feel they are active contributors to the solution. In your role as the organizational leader, you must work to involve the group as a whole in order to create meaningful learning experiences and connectedness for members of the group.

Additionally, looking at this case through the psychosocial lens could provide conversations about personal development. The work of Chickering and Reisser (1993), Erickson (1980), and Josselson (1996), to cite a few, would provide the opportunity to look at not only personal development, but also the individual in relation to others and how their roles in the group are defined by that relationship. Alternatively, if you use a cognitive development lens, it would give insight into how individuals are thinking about their role in the group. Cognitive development theorists such as Perry (1970), Kegan (1998), and Baxter Magolda (2001) and the work of Belenky, Clinchy, Goldberger, and Tarule (1997) examine how students make decisions based on the complexity of their thought processes. Higher-level thinkers have the ability to analyze situations and make decisions based on their internal sense of self, rather than external authorities. Through a cognitive lens, you, as the group leader, may be able to explain more thoroughly why certain individuals are unwilling to think differently about activities.

Another important body of scholarship to consider during the analysis of these cases is leadership development theory. The social change model of leadership development (Higher Education Research Institute, 1996), the relational leadership model (Komives, Lucas, & McMahon, 2007), and the servant leadership approach (Greenleaf, 1977) all provide an approach to analyze the cases with an emphasis on the leader's role. The leadership challenge model (Kouzes & Posner, 2002) provides a list of competencies based on extensive research related to best practices in leadership development. This growing body of literature cuts across many academic disciplines and plays an important role in understanding and facilitating the leadership development of college students.

**Do our organizations ever get so entrenched in tradition that we lose creativity?**

There are multiple ways to approach this question as the facilitator. Using the issues in the present case, the answer may be yes for the group. The unwillingness of some of the group members to think differently about activities seems to point out that this group has become very entrenched in tradition. As the leader, you can illustrate that diversifying activities and party themes may engage individuals who may not otherwise participate. This gives the group the opportunity to diversify membership.

In working with the freshman and sophomore students and their desire to preserve the past, as the group leader you should think about why they are struggling. Their inability to be creative and think about the needs and desires of others in the group is developmentally appropriate. Through the lens of gender identity development, theorists Gilligan (1993), Davis (2002), and Josselson (1996) discuss how individuals use external groups and people to construct their sense of self early in their college tenure. As students grow and have a variety of experiences in college, their sense of who they are and how they define themselves changes and becomes more internal.

Next, the juniors and seniors in this case may be more interested in changing existing programs because they do not define themselves by the organization; rather, the organization is part of them. Juniors and seniors sometimes have the ability to be less connected to the organization. This is a natural part of growth and development through college. In addition, senior-level students usually begin to move on to other activities, and their investment in the organization changes over time. It is difficult for freshmen and sophomores to understand this natural development because of their limited development perspective.

**Do you talk about the varying needs of your constituents? How does your organization meet the needs of all its members? Do you create goals for your organization and challenge each other to come up with something new that meets the needs of your various members?**

As the group leader, it is important that you work to maintain a balance with all your constituents. Groups cannot meet all needs for all members. In the analysis of these questions, it is important that the theories addressing psychosocial, cognitive, and gender identity be employed in the discussion. Each body of theories can serve as a set of tools for understanding why students may respond differently to a case. As the facilitator, it is essential that you use these theories as guideposts for understanding and challenging your students and interpreting their responses.

## SUMMARY

The preceding case was analyzed using a variety of student development theories. It is important to remember that there are many theories that can be used for analysis. Some theories are more appropriate for cases than others, but how students make meaning of the issues needs to be analyzed using a theoretical lens.

The use of theories in case-study analysis gives legitimacy to our work and profession. We have many empirically based theories that help to explain how students make decisions, work through issues on campus, and make sense of the college environment. Therefore, we should apply these theories to inform our students' interpretation of the cases. It is ethically appropriate to ground these discussions in a theoretical framework balanced with the appreciation that all students are individuals.

Finally, there are many other student development theories that were not cited in this case analysis. For example, for literature that addresses how students develop identity based on race, see Helms (1990), Hardiman (1982), Phinney (1989), Cross (1971), and Ortiz and Rhoads (2000). For cases based on issues of identity as related to sexual orientation, see D'Augelli (1994) and Cass (1979). When students are exploring aspects of their spiritual and moral development, see Fowler (1981), Parks (1986), Kohlberg (1981), and King and Kitchener (1994). In addition, there are other disciplines that address development across the life span and these may be appropriate in the analysis of cases related to college students.

# REFERENCES

Astin, A. W. (1984). Student involvement: A developmental theory for higher education. *Journal of College Student Personnel, 25,* 297–302.

Baxter Magolda, M. B. (2001). *Making their own way: Narratives for transforming higher education to promote self-development.* Sterling, VA: Stylus.

Belenky, M., Clinchy, B., Goldberger, N. R., & Tarule, J. (1997). *Women's ways of knowing: The development of self, mind, and voice.* New York: Basic Books.

Cass, V. (1979). Homosexual identity formation: A theoretical model. *Journal of Homosexuality, 4,* 219–235.

Chickering, A. W., & Reisser, L. (1993). *Education and identity.* San Francisco: Jossey-Bass.

Cross, W. E. (1971). The Negro-to-Black conversion experience. *Black World, 20,* 13–26.

D'Augelli, A. R. (1994). Identity development and sexual orientation: Toward a model of lesbian, gay, and bisexual development. In E. J. Trickett, R. J. Watts, & D. Birman (Eds.), *Human diversity: Perspectives on people in context* (pp. 312–333). San Francisco: Jossey-Bass.

Davis, T. L. (2002). Voices of gender role conflict: The social construction of college men's identity. *Journal of College Student Development, 43,* 508–521.

Erickson, E. H. (1980). *Identity and the life cycle.* New York: W.W. Norton.

Fowler, J. W. (1981). *Stages of faith: The psychology of human development and the quest for meaning.* San Francisco: HarperCollins.

Gilligan, C. (1993). *In a different voice: Psychological theory and women's development.* Cambridge, MA: Harvard University Press.

Greenleaf, R. G. (1977). *Servant leadership: A journey in the nature of legitimate power and greatness.* New York: Paulist Press.

Hardiman, R. (1982). *White identity development: A process oriented model for describing the racial consciousness of White Americans.* Unpublished doctoral dissertation. University of Massachusetts, Amherst.

Helms, J. E. (1990). *Black and White racial identity: Theory, research, and practice.* Westport, CT: Greenwood Press.

Higher Education Research Institute. (1996). *Collaborative leadership for social change—guidebook (Version III).* Los Angeles: UCLA Higher Education Research Institute

Josselson, R. E. (1996). *Identity.* Oxford, England: Oxford University Press.

Kegan, R. (1998). *In over our heads: The mental demands of modern life.* Cambridge, MA: Harvard University Press.

King, P. M., & Kitchener, K. S. (1994). *Developing reflective judgment: Understanding and promoting intellectual growth and critical thinking in adolescents and adults.* San Francisco: Jossey-Bass.

Kohlberg, L. (1981). *The meaning and measurement of moral development.* Worcester, MA: Clark University Press.

Komives, S. R., Lucas, N., & McMahon, T. R. (2007). *Exploring leadership: For college students who want to make a difference* (2nd ed.). San Francisco: Jossey-Bass.

Kouzes, J. M., & Posner, B. Z. (2002). *The leadership challenge* (3rd ed.). San Francisco: Jossey-Bass.

Kuh, G. D., Kinzie, J., Schuh, J. H., Whitt, E. J., & Associates. (2005). *Student success in college: Creating conditions that matter.* San Francisco: Jossey-Bass.

Magolda, P. M. (2001). What our campus rituals tell us about community on campus: A look at the campus tour. *About Campus, 5*(6), 2–8.

Ortiz, A. M., & Rhoads, R. A. (2000). Deconstructing Whiteness as part of a multicultural educational framework. *Journal of College Student Development, 41,* 81–93.

Parks, S. (1986). *The critical years: Young adults and the search for meaning, faith, and commitment.* San Francisco: HarperCollins.

Perry, W. G. (1970). *Forms of intellectual and ethical development in the college years.* New York: Holt, Rinehart & Winston.

Phinney, J. (1989). Stages of ethnic identity in minority group adolescents. *Journal of Early Adolescence, 9,* 34–49.

# 3

# RESIDENCE LIFE CASES
# APPROPRIATE FOR
# RESIDENT ADVISORS

## ROOMMATE CONFLICTS

### Roommate Abuse

As a resident assistant (RA) you share a suite with two other roommates. Although you have your own room, you share a common living area and a bathroom. This is the living arrangement for all the RAs in your building. One of your roommates, Jim, begins dating Emily, another resident in your building who shares a room with another RA, Sandy. Jim and Emily's relationship continues to develop and soon you start to witness that Jim is becoming more and more verbally abusive of Emily while in your presence. You ask Sandy if she has witnessed similar abuse. She says she has heard Jim verbally abuse Emily, and she has even seen him forcefully grab Emily's arm but has not done anything about it.

- What are the issues in this case?
- What are your options for handling the situation? How might each option play out? Which option do you prefer?

- How will you address the behavior? What will you say to Jim? Will you do so in front of Emily? Will you talk with Emily separately?
- What should you do if you learn that you are the only RA confronting the behavior? What should you do if Jim gets angry with you when you confront him and says that Sandy has never said anything?
- Keep in mind that you have to live with Jim, and Sandy with Emily. Does this alter your approach to the situation? Would you handle things differently if Jim weren't your roommate?

## Different Forms of Communication

Two roommates on your floor do not get along. They seem to disagree on nearly everything. One goes to bed early, and one stays up late. One listens to music, and the other prefers television. One studies a lot, and the other loves to socialize at all hours of the night. You have already sat down with them once to complete a roommate agreement form. At the time, they agreed to compromise on a variety of issues so that the living environment would be suitable for both. However, slowly, over time, the two started to deviate from the signed agreement. Rather than discuss their problems face-to-face, they e-mail and instant message (IM) each other. The e-mails and IMs get nastier over the course of several weeks. One of the roommates comes to you to learn how to break his housing contract. You ask the student if he has talked with his roommate about the problems and revisited the signed agreement. He admits that they talk electronically and that things have taken a turn for the worse.

- What are the issues in this case?
- What are your options for handling the situation? How might each option play out? Which option do you prefer?
- How will you respond to this resident? Should you give him the information to break his contract? Should you discuss any alternatives? Should you send him back to talk face-to-face to his roommate? Are you involved or is he on his own?
- Should you have followed up on the roommate agreement to make sure the students were adhering to it and getting along? If so, how often should an RA follow up?

- At what point is a room change or release of contract necessary? When should an RA help a student get out of a bad situation versus encourage him or her to learn from the experience?
- What lessons can the residents learn from this experience? Can additional communication help them?
- What is the RA's role in this conflict? Should he or she even care? What should you do if this is your fourth roommate conflict this week and you are tired and find yourself wondering, "When will these residents start to fend for themselves?"?

## You Don't Celebrate Halloween?

Four residents are assigned to a two-bedroom apartment. Two juniors lived in the room last year and elected to live in the same apartment their senior year. Two sophomores signed up to live in the same apartment to fill the quad. The two seniors are African American and are good friends. The two sophomores are White and also are good friends. Prior to moving in, the two seniors do not know the two sophomores. Conflict quickly arises as the seniors move in first and promptly "take over" most of the common living space. They communicate with the sophomores that this is their second year in the same apartment and that last year they "ran off" the other two roommates so they could have the apartment all to themselves. The sophomores are eager to make the living arrangements work because they know that if they move out the only alternative will be to live in a traditional-style residence hall with community bathrooms. Campus apartments are highly sought after and they feel very fortunate to have obtained one as sophomores. As the semester progresses, the seniors continue to make the living arrangements unbearable. They eat the sophomores' food, borrow their things without permission, have guests at all hours, and do not clean up after themselves. The sophomores become increasingly angry and offended by the actions of their roommates. They talk with their RA multiple times and complete two roommate agreements. Nothing changes. The final straw comes when the sophomores hang Halloween decorations in the apartment and put out a dish of candy only to come home later that day to find that the seniors have torn down all the decorations and thrown away the candy.

When confronted, the seniors say, "Halloween is sacrilegious and against our religion. We think these decorations are offensive and will not permit them in our living space." The sophomores have had it! They want the seniors *out!* Of course, both groups dislike the living arrangement, yet neither will agree to move out and give up the apartment.

When you meet with the four roommates, the seniors claim that the sophomores are just disrespectful. They prank call them, leave nasty messages, don't clean up after themselves, eat their food, have visitors in the apartment at all hours, and are just as guilty of creating an unlivable environment. Parents from both sides start calling you, and your hall director demands immediate action.

- What are the issues in this case?
- What are your options for handling the situation? How might each option play out? Which option do you prefer?
- Whom do you believe? Who is at fault? Does it matter that one group is seniors and the other sophomores? Does race influence your reaction/response?
- How should you proceed? What should you do if you can't prove that the seniors "ran off" last year's roommates? What should you do if you can prove it? What should you do if the seniors think you are discriminating against them because they are African American?

## Don't Do Anything

Lemont, an African American student living on your residence-hall floor, is not liked by his three White roommates. Throughout the semester the animosity toward Lemont escalates. Late one Thursday night, someone paints on Lemont's door, "I can't stand coons." Lemont is confident that his roommates are responsible for the act. He tells you, the RA, "I don't want to do anything about this because it will only make things worse for me. It's really no big deal. I'll just wash it off and we'll forget about it." You know as an RA that you must file an incident report.

- What are the issues in this case?
- What are your options for handling the situation? How might each option play out? Which option do you prefer?

- How will you address the situation with the roommates?
- Since most of your residents know about the incident, how will you address it with your floor?

## INTERSTAFF CONFLICTS

## Stepping Up

As a residence hall staff member, you are required to facilitate a buildingwide program each month. Your hall director puts you into groups of three and assigns your group approximately one program per month for the entire school year. You are to work collaboratively to coordinate the programs and share the responsibility for their implementation. Month after month, you end up coordinating 90 percent of the required program. Your fellow RAs tell you they will do something but routinely drop the ball. This means that you have to pick up the slack and do most of the work in order for the program to be a success. You have talked to them once about doing more and they both apologized but reminded you that they had major tests, other organization commitments, or family emergencies that took them away from their responsibilities. They also said how they really appreciate how you have helped cover for them.

- What are the issues in this case?
- What are your options for handling the situation? How might each option play out? Which option do you prefer?
- How do you plan to address this situation? Will you continue to shoulder most of the programming burden? Do you let a program fail?
- At what point should you get your hall director involved? Will involving the hall director cause conflict within the group? Will you be viewed as a "tattletale"?
- Can you think of times when you or someone else did all the work and the "team" got the credit? How have you handled these situations? Did you say something?

# The Rambler

Stephanie is one of the RAs on your staff. Your hall director is brand new and is still learning. Since Stephanie has been an RA in your building for the past three years, she has deemed herself the expert. She lets the rest of the staff know that she has seen it all and confronted it all. In your weekly staff meetings she likes to talk. She tends to dominate the discussion, tells others what to do, and is often the resident historian. She often halts progress by saying things like, "Well, we used to do things this way" or "We have always done it this way." The staff quickly tires of her domination and the hall director is not doing anything to stop it. If anything, she tends to defer to Stephanie when she does not know the answer or appropriate action. The staff is quickly getting frustrated and losing confidence in its hall director. You are a second-year RA and a respected member of the staff. The rest of the RAs ask you do something about the current situation.

- What are the issues in this case?
- What are your options for handling the situation? How might each option play out? Which option do you prefer?
- How do you respond to the RAs' request? Is it your responsibility to confront the situation?
- What are your options? Do you choose to do nothing? Do you talk with the hall director? Do you talk with Stephanie? What do you say to them? Do you report back to the staff?

# Do Your Job!

It is almost the end of the school year, only one month to go. The RA staff includes two sophomores, four juniors, and three graduating seniors. You hear through the grapevine that two of the seniors are starting to slack on their RA duties. When on duty, they are not doing full rounds and even skip the 1:00 A.M. rounds. A resident comes to you and tells you that one of the senior RAs was drinking with a group of residents the night before.

- What are the issues in this case?
- What are your options for handling the situation? How might each option play out? Which option do you prefer?

- How do you respond to the resident? Do you have any recommendations for the resident?
- What are your options for handling the issue with the two graduating RAs? Do you handle it at all? Would you handle it differently if you were the third senior and a good friend of the others?
- What should you do if you confront them and they tell you that they don't care anymore and just want to enjoy the rest of their senior year?

## Who's the Boss?

Your hall director is very experienced. For the past six years, she has served as the hall director in your building. She will be the first to tell you that she has seen it all. She knows the flow of the academic year, the type of resident issues that will arise, and what programs are most successful. She knows how to run the building and what works. She makes it obvious that she is in charge and is the expert. Although the new RA staff members appreciate her wisdom in the beginning of the school year, they are also a bit intimidated by her. The RAs rely on her a great deal as they learn how to interact with their residents, confront policy violations, and plan their first programs.

As the year progresses and the RAs become more confident in their roles, they become more independent and start to generate new ideas for the building. However, the hall director politely squashes each new idea. She uses language such as, "Oh, that just won't work in this building" or "We can try it, but I really think we should stick with what has worked historically." At first, the staff members concede, but eventually they start to resent that their opinions and ideas are not valued by their supervisor. You are a returning RA and appreciate your hall director. You know that she can be difficult at times but that deep down she is only doing what is best for the residents.

- What are the issues in this case?
- What are your options for handling the situation? How might each option play out? Which option do you prefer?
- How do you approach your hall director? Do you talk with the rest of the staff?

- What do you think will happen if you don't do anything? How bad should you let things get before stepping in? Whose role is it to say or do something?

## Is It Really Love?

Sam is a second-year-graduate hall director at Central Eastern University (CEU). He supervises eight RAs in an upper-class residence hall, Kendall Hall. Three of the eight staff members are returning RAs, including Katie, who is a senior at CEU. Sam is pursuing a master's degree in student affairs administration at CEU. He decided to pursue his master's and a career in student affairs immediately following completion of his bachelor's degree. Sam is twenty-three years old. Early in the fall Sam and Katie secretly start dating. They know it is against residence life policy for hall directors to date RAs, but their attraction for each other can no longer be denied. They date for the entire first semester and it slowly becomes common knowledge among the Kendall Hall staff. Most are indifferent about their relationship. They know that they are breaking policy but don't say anything. After winter break, the staff returns for training and discovers that Katie and Sam broke off their relationship over the break. It was obviously a bad breakup because they can hardly stand to be in the same room together. The tension that this creates leads the staff to start taking sides based on whose story about the breakup—Sam's or Katie's—they believe.

- What are the issues in this case?
- What are the options for handling the situation? How might each option play out? Which option do you prefer?
- Do you think it is appropriate for a hall director and an RA to date each other? What about two RAs? What about an RA and his or her resident? Where do you draw the line?
- Would you approve of the relationship if it was serious and they planned to get married?
- How does interstaff dating impact the dynamics of a residence hall team?

# Unfair Treatment

Jim is the hall director of Standish Hall. He's been the hall director of this building for the past three years. Although he hired his residence hall staff, it quickly becomes obvious that he dislikes Raul, a first-year RA. He criticizes Raul in front of the rest of the staff for turning in his paperwork late but doesn't criticize the others who do the same thing. He criticizes Raul for how he handles confrontation, plans programs for his floor, and interacts with the rest of the staff. Jim also talks negatively about Raul to the other residence life staff members. Similarly, Raul talks about his frustration with Jim with the other staff members. The staff is frustrated and begins to choose sides. No one knows why Jim is so hard on Raul. Some speculate that it is because he is Hispanic. Although Raul is an effective RA, at the end of the first semester he is ready to quit. He tells you, as the senior RA, that he can't take it anymore. He just doesn't understand why Jim doesn't like him.

- What are the issues in this case?
- What are your options for handling the situation? How might each option play out? Which option do you prefer?
- What might happen if you do or say nothing?
- Should Raul say anything to Jim about how he really feels? If he tells Jim that he thinks his race is a factor, will Jim think that he's pulling the "race card"?
- As the senior RA, what should you say to Raul? Should you talk with Jim? Should you have said something to Raul earlier in the semester?
- Should Raul quit?

# Ready to Be an RA?

One of your best friends wants to be an RA. She claims that she really needs the money and the free housing in order to stay in school for another year. Although she is one of your good friends, you know that she isn't the most responsible person in the world. She misses deadlines and isn't great with follow-through. She is also very kind and you fear that she would have a tough time handling the discipline portion of the job. A member of the RA selection committee knows that she is a friend of yours and asks you for your opinion of her.

- What are the issues in this case?
- What are your options for handling the situation? How might each option play out? Which option do you prefer?
- Should you do what is best for your friend or what is best for the department?
- Should you be honest with your friend?

## Skipping Class

RA George has a class with many of his residents. The class meets two times per week and he typically skips class at least once a week. His residents continually joke about how during their first hall meeting he lectured them about the importance of attending class. They tell you, another RA in the building, about George's lack of attendance in class and about how he is the butt of their jokes.

- What are the issues in this case?
- What are your options for handling the situation? How might each option play out? Which option do you prefer?
- Is it possible that there is some reason why George is missing class?
- When is an RA simply a student and when is an RA a role model for his or her residents?
- If George continually asks his residents for class notes, should they help him? What should you do if he's skipping class because he parties the night before and is too hung over to attend?

## STUDENT DISCIPLINE CASES

## Is It All about the Marijuana?

You notice that one of your residents, Bill, is frequently skipping class. Bill's roommate comes to you and tells you that Bill sleeps most of the day. He then says, "There is something else going on with him but I can't tell you unless you promise not to tell anyone or bust him for it." You agree and the roommate informs you that Bill smokes marijuana multiple times a day. You like Bill; he is a good guy. You also feel caught by your promise to Bill's roommate. You can't confront Bill or write him up. You decide to watch his room closely and confront any suspect behavior. Within two days you notice a strange smell emanating from Bill's room at about 1:30 A.M. You are confident that what you smell is marijuana. You knock on the door and identify yourself. You hear shuffling and Bill asks you to wait a minute. You tell Bill to open the door immediately. He opens the door and you ask him what he's doing. He is disoriented and his pupils are dilated. You scan the room and notice drug paraphernalia in a half-open drawer. You inquire about the items and again about his actions. He admits that he was smoking a little weed to relax. Although Bill pleads with you not to do anything, you call campus police and write up the incident. The next day Bill comes to your room and apologizes for his actions the night before. He becomes very emotional as he tells you that he's under a great deal of pressure from his family, especially his father, to be like his older brother. His brother is a great athlete, he's on the dean's list, and he's an all-around great guy. Bill explains that he smokes pot to escape the pressure.

- What are the issues in this case?
- What are your options for handling the situation? How might each option play out? Which option do you prefer?
- Did you do the right thing by reporting the incident?
- What are the next steps to help Bill? Should you follow up with his roommate? Does someone need to talk with Bill's father?

## Poker, Anyone?

A group of six residents meets each week for a game of poker. The stakes are relatively small, with dollar bets, dollar antes, and a three-bet limit. One resident, Kerry, seems particularly interested in the game. He asks his buddies to increase the limit and tries to get them to play more than once a week. He also starts gambling at the local casino multiple times per week. His roommate tells you that Kerry is online investigating sports scores a great deal of the time and may be gambling on sports using the Internet. While his gambling seems to be escalating, the university does not have a policy that prohibits gambling on campus. You tell yourself, "The poker games are harmless; all the residents are really into poker and Texas hold 'em. The other gambling he's doing is off campus, so what can I really do about it, anyway?" You decide to keep an eye on Kerry but convince yourself that there is nothing you can do. About a month later, your residents start reporting the theft of various items, including an iPod, DVDs, and cash.

- What are the issues in this case?
- What are your options for handling the situation? How might each option play out? Which option do you prefer?
- What is your initial reaction to the recent string of thefts? Could they be in any way related to Kerry's gambling?
- Should you address the situation? If so, how?
- When does gambling become a problem? An addiction? A policy violation?

## No Friend of Mine

Susan is a junior and a first-year RA. She is the RA in an upper-class, coed apartment building. Because many juniors live in the apartments, most of Susan's residents are also her friends. Her first night on duty, Susan has to confront a noise complaint in the apartment of one of her friends. She knocks on the door and quickly discovers that there are fifteen people in the apartment, most of whom are under age. She also sees several cases of beer. Julie, her friend who lives in the apartment, is relieved to see that it is Susan. She welcomes her into the room and apologizes for the noise. Julie and her guests offer Susan a beer. When Susan tries to address the situation by collecting IDs and asking Julie to dispose of the alcohol, Julie becomes angry. She says, "Come on, Susan! You can't be serious. You party with us all the time. I thought you were going to be a cool RA. You aren't going to write us up, are you? You can't!" However, Susan does exactly that. She sees Julie the next day and Julie won't even look at her. Susan feels all sorts of emotions: she feels guilty about busting her friends, angry about having to bust her friends, and sad that she might have lost some friends. She's left thinking, "Maybe this job isn't all that it's cracked up to be."

- What are the issues in this case?
- What are Susan's options for handling the situation? How might each option play out? Which option do you prefer?
- What would you tell Susan? Should she have let her friends off with a warning?
- How should Susan handle her friendship with Julie given the write-up?
- Is it possible to be both a resident's friend and an RA?

## No Jumping in the Elevators

During the first week of school, residents are told not to jump in the elevators, because this may cause the elevators to break down. A group of residents decide to ignore the policy and jump in unison in an elevator. Consequently, the elevator breaks down and they are trapped. They pry the doors open about five inches and can see residents on the floor above. They call for help and you are the closest staff member. You call for a repair person, but it will take about an hour for the person to arrive. You are able to communicate with the residents in the elevator. One trapped resident says she is starting to panic, another says she feels like she's going to vomit, and another says she has to use the bathroom.

- What are the issues in this case?
- What are your options for handling the situation? How might each option play out? Which option do you prefer?
- How would you keep the residents calm and attend to their needs?
- Should you write up the incident after they are released?

## SITUATIONS WITH PARENTS

## Drug Distribution

On move-in day, Sheila's mother approaches you. She hands you her daughter's antidepressant medication and gives you instructions for administering it to her daughter.

- What are the issues in this case?
- What are your options for handling the situation? How might each option play out? Which option do you prefer? Keep in mind that Sheila's mother has always given Sheila her medication. Sheila tends not to keep track of time, and if she is made responsible for taking her medication, it is highly unlikely that she will medicate herself appropriately.

## Who's Dating My Son?

You return from class and find a message on your answering machine from Trevor's dad. Trevor is one of your first-year residents. His father insists that you call him immediately because he wants to know if his son's girlfriend has been staying over. He also wants to know if Trevor's girlfriend is White. You are surprised by the call. Trevor is African American and you know that Trevor is dating Emily, a White woman.

- What are the issues in this case?
- What are your options for handling the situation? How might each option play out? Which option do you prefer?
- What should you do if you approach Trevor and he agrees to talk to his dad but then never does? What should you do if Trevor's dad continues to call you because Trevor tells him that he's not dating anyone but his dad believes that he is?

## Just Drinking with My Kid

It is about 6:00 P.M. on move-in day. There is a picnic in the quad for all new students. As you visit all your residents' rooms to invite them to the picnic, you notice that two sets of parents are still in their children's room. The roommates are high school friends. When you approach the room, you see that the parents and their kids (your underage residents) are drinking beer.

- What are the issues in this case?
- What are your options for handling the situation? How might each option play out? Which option do you prefer?
- If you decide to confront the situation, what should you do if the parents become angry? What should you do if the parents are alumni and claim that they used to have big keg parties and have all kinds of fun and that the school has become really uptight?
- If you decide not to confront the situation, what message will you be sending your residents?

## Condoms, Ten for a Dollar

The university health center sells ten condoms for a dollar. They make the sale of condoms affordable and convenient for college students in an effort to reduce the number of unwanted pregnancies and the spread of sexually transmitted diseases. You hang one of the health center's promotional flyers on your door along with many other promotional ads. One of the parents reads the condom flyer and confronts you. A conservative, religious man, he is irate that you are encouraging promiscuity. He cannot believe that the school would condone the sale of condoms and demands that you take the flyer down.

- What are the issues in this case?
- What are your options for handling the situation? How might each option play out? Which option do you prefer?

## Check Me Out Now!

It is the end of the year and residents are required to sign up for checkout appointments with their RA. They must do this at least twenty-four hours before their checkout time in order to give the RA enough time to make himself or herself available. Stephanie signs up at 3:00 A.M. for a 7:00 A.M. checkout. She and her father knock on your door at 7:00 A.M. waking you up and demanding that you check her out. Stephanie has been a high-maintenance resident all year. She has been demanding, critical, and a negative influence on the floor. Now, her father is very demanding with you as well, and you can't help thinking to yourself, "I guess the apple doesn't fall far from the tree."

- What are the issues in this case?
- What are your options for handling the situation? How might each option play out? Which option do you prefer?
- Does your opinion of the resident influence your willingness to help her? What would you do if another resident for whom you have a high regard did the same thing?
- Does the presence of Stephanie's father influence your response? How would you respond if he were not present?

# I Only Took a Sip

Five residents are caught drinking and smoking on an alcohol- and tobacco-free floor. At the beginning of the school year, all residents signed a form agreeing that they would not drink or smoke on the floor. They also agreed to hold each other accountable. The five residents caught breaking the agreement will go through the conduct system, and if they are found responsible they will be placed on social probation and pay a fifty-dollar fine. One of the residents' mothers calls and pleads with you not to report her daughter. Her daughter told her that she only had a sip of alcohol and shouldn't be fined like the others.

- What are the issues in this case?
- What are your options for handling the situation? How might each option play out? Which option do you prefer?
- Does the mother's call influence how you would handle the situation? Would you handle the situation differently if the daughter told you she felt a great deal of peer pressure to drink with the group?

# Let Me In

One of your residents, Jackson, and his dad knock on your door on a Sunday night. Jackson's dad informs you that Jackson left his room key at home and tells you to key Jackson into his room until he can mail the key to his son.

- What are the issues in this case?
- What are your options for handling the situation? How might each option play out? Which option do you prefer?
- How would you handle the situation if Jackson's dad had been kinder and asked you to let Jackson in his room instead of demanding that you do so?

# A Quick Errand

On move-in day you sense that a resident is going to be high maintenance when carpet layers begin installing wall-to-wall carpet. Early in the day, the resident's mother comes to you and asks you to make a quick run to the local hardware store to pick up a few items for her daughter's room.

- What are the issues in this case?
- What are your options for handling the situation? How might each option play out? Which option do you prefer?
- What would you do if you were currently off duty and the resident's father offered to pay you fifty dollars to run the errand?

# There's a Lesbian in My Daughter's Room

The mother of one of your residents calls you one afternoon and demands that you make her daughter's roommate move out. She informs you that she checked out the roommate's Facebook page and learned that she prefers same-sex relationships. The mother insists that her daughter cannot live with a lesbian. The mother thinks that all the lesbians on campus should live together.

- What are the issues in this case?
- What are your options for handling the situation? How might each option play out? Which option do you prefer?
- What should you do if the mother hasn't talked with her daughter? What should you do if the mother has talked with her daughter and the daughter also wants another roommate?
- Why do you think the mother wants to inconvenience the roommate?

## MISCELLANEOUS RESIDENT ISSUES

## Whom Do I Call?

As the RA in a brand-new residence hall, you feel that the training and preparation for the position was short and inadequate. You have nothing to compare it to, but in conversations with your friends at other schools, you find that they had a more extensive orientation. The first semester goes by with no incidents. You have to write up a few alcohol violations and a few noise complaints but nothing too major.

During the first week of the second semester, however, Renee, a resident on your floor, pounds on your door and tells you that Cathy, her roommate, has taken a whole bottle of pills and is lying on the floor. On the way to your room, Renee yells all the way down the hall, and many of the other women on the floor open their doors and ask what is going on. You call 911 and campus public safety but are not sure what else to do.

- What are the issues in this case?
- What are your options for handling the situation? How might each option play out? Which option do you prefer?
- How should you proceed? Whom should you involve in helping you handle the situation?

## Stripper in the Lounge

Tuesday evening in Ledding Hall is usually slow, but on February 12 the night is hopping. It begins with complaints about noise on the fourth floor and an alcohol party on the first floor and ends with a complaint about a stripper in the second-floor lounge. Around 8:00 P.M., a female student comes running down to your office and says that four men have a stripper in the second-floor lounge. This lounge happens to be in the female wing of the floor. By the time you get to the lounge, the four men have been joined by six additional students and there are two strippers, instead of just one. You clear out the lounge and begin taking names from the men in the room.

- What are the issues in this case?
- What are your options for handling the situation? How might each option play out? Which option do you prefer?
- How should the hall director proceed with disciplinary actions?

## Too Thin

Diedra, a female resident, informs you, as her RA, that she has lupus. She wants to make you aware because she has some special needs and uncommon eating patterns. She cannot eat and has to use a feeding tube for nourishment. She believes that she has her disease under control and does not want the other residents on her floor to know. Diedra is very thin. During the first semester, three female residents ask to meet with you because they are concerned that Diedra may have an eating disorder. They never see her eat and they believe that she is too thin.

- What are the issues in this case?
- What are your options for handling the situation? How might each option play out? Which option do you prefer?
- How would Diedra feel if you disclosed her disease? What should you do if Diedra continues to not want anyone to know, despite the concerns of her fellow residents?
- Is it possible that Diedra has an eating disorder in addition to lupus?

# Flirting with the RA

You are a male junior in a predominantly first-year building. Although you have a girlfriend, your female residents keep hitting on you. They continually IM you, they frequently stop in to "ask a question," and some are even bold enough to ask you out. Although you keep telling them that it is against the rules to date residents and that you have a girlfriend, they keep flirting with you. You really like being an RA, but your girlfriend insists that you finish the school year and not return for a second year.

- What are the issues in this case?
- What are your options for handling the situation? How might each option play out? Which option do you prefer?
- If another RA had the same problem, what advice would you offer him or her?
- Do you think your own behavior sends mixed messages to your residents and your girlfriend?

# My Parents Can't Handle the Fact That I'm Bisexual

Resident Elise is bisexual. Two weeks before winter break, she "comes out" to her family. Her mother is terminally ill and her brother is in the seminary. Upon her return to campus, she tells you that her family basically disowned her when she informed them of her sexual orientation. She is a bit worried because she doesn't have a place to stay for winter break. Internally she is very upset about their negative reaction, but when she's around her floor mates she acts as if her family's reaction to her bisexuality is no big deal. She starts drinking excessively, and one night while drunk she is belligerent to one of the RAs. The RA writes her up. Later that week she drinks to the point that she passes out in the bathroom.

- What are the issues in this case?
- What are your options for handling the situation? How might each option play out? Which option do you prefer?
- Regarding Elise's excessive drinking, at what point should you suspect alcohol poisoning and call an ambulance?
- Should there be any intervention with Elise's parents?

# A Cutter

Transfer student Valerie is a cutter. She transferred from the local community college and you've been worried about her since the start of the school year. She informs you that she has a lot of problems. Her parents are divorced. She has trouble maintaining relationships and admits to having multiple miscarriages. She sometimes turns to drugs and alcohol to forget about the troubles in her life. Although she tells you her problems, she doesn't want help. You make counseling appointments for her but she doesn't show up. You also walk her to the counseling center but she refuses to talk with a counselor when she gets there. You now notice marks on her arms and realize that she is cutting herself.

- What are the issues in this case?
- What are your options for handling the situation? How might each option play out? Which option do you prefer?
- Would Valerie really tell you her problems if she didn't want help? Why do you think she disclosed all this information to you?
- What is your responsibility to Valerie? How much time do you dedicate to one resident even if it means neglecting your other residents?
- What should you do if the cutting gets worse? At what point is it no longer safe for Valerie to live in the residence hall? What should you do if her cutting negatively impacts the residents on your floor? For example, some residents are preoccupied with her cutting or are worried because there is blood in the bathroom or some residents want to help her whereas others want her off the floor.

# Whose Side?

You are the RA for a coed floor. On Saturday night a male and a female resident get drunk. Later that evening the female resident is allegedly raped by the male resident. She doesn't go to the hospital but does fill out an incident report. He claims that the sex was consensual and cannot believe that she is calling him a rapist. The floor residents learn of the incident and quickly take sides. They cannot stop talking about the incident.

- What are the issues in this case?
- What are your options for handling the situation? How might each option play out? Which option do you prefer?
- What should you do if you personally believe one resident over the other? What is your obligation to both residents?
- If you suggest that one resident move off the floor, what should you do if neither one will move?
- What should you do if the aggression on the floor escalates and someone vandalizes the woman's door by painting a derogatory remark on it?

# Overdose

Ramon is a student from Africa. He has been in the United States for two years and hopes to stay here for the rest of his life. His home country is in turmoil and he dreads the thought of possibly having to return. He has been working in the campus cafeteria but was recently fired because he missed work multiple times. Because he lost his job he can no longer afford to stay in the States. His biggest fear is that he will be sent back to his home country. For two weeks he looks for another job, but nothing is available, and many are hesitant to hire a foreign student. He gets more and more depressed. One night he swallows a bottle of sleeping pills. His roommates find him and he admits that he took the pills. The roommates come to you and explain what Ramon has done, and you call for an ambulance. Ramon is transported to the hospital, where the doctors pump his stomach. When he returns to the residence hall, he is angry because now he has an expensive hospital bill on top of everything else.

- What are the issues in this case?
- What are your options for handling the situation? How might each option play out? Which option do you prefer?
- Do you have any obligation to help Ramon find a job or a way to offset his growing debt?

# I Need You

Alice is one of your favorite residents. You would even consider her your friend. She comes to you and tells you that she is pregnant. She also tells you that her parents will kill her if they find out that she is pregnant and that the father was a one-night stand. Having the baby really isn't an option. She has considered all of her options and plans to have an abortion. She asks you to go with her to the medical appointment. There is no one else she can ask and she doesn't want to go alone. You are against abortion but you know that Alice needs you.

- What are the issues in this case?
- What are your options for handling the situation? How might each option play out? Which option do you prefer?
- When do you compromise your own beliefs to support a resident?
- Are you obligated to inform anyone about the abortion? Your hall director? Alice's parents?

# To Tell or Not to Tell

Roman is a sophomore living in Bass Academic House. Bass House is an off-campus house for male students on full academic scholarships. The Bass family donated a large sum of money to Disney University for scholarships as well as for room and board. The university holds a competition once a year to determine the recipient. Competitors come from fifteen high schools in the geographic area. The daylong competition includes an academic piece and an athletic component. Roman earned the scholarship last year and has been living in Bass House for one year. Since the house is governed by the university, freshmen can live in the house instead of the residence halls.

Roman has earned the reputation of being a leader in the house. He is handy, neat, and an all-around good housemate. He put together a group last year who redid the landscaping in the front yard. He also has helped paint and remodel four of the bedrooms in the house. His parents even donated some old sofas and tables so that the men could have nicer furnishings in the living room.

The requirements for living in the house and keeping the scholarship are that students must maintain a grade point average (GPA) above 2.5 and be enrolled in at least fifteen semester credit hours. The responsibility of seeing that students maintain these requirements from year to year falls on the president of Bass Academic House. The house is considered a registered student organization and because of its size operates like a residence hall on campus. Ralph is the president but he is not the best at following through. He is a good student and a member of the varsity water polo team. He attends all house meetings but does little else around the house. He is well liked by the other members of the house, so his behavior is tolerated. During the third week of each new semester, Ralph is to review the grade reports for all the Bass House students. This is an important job because the Bass family has made it very clear that the expectations set out in the agreement must be followed. Ralph always gives the report a cursory review and for two semesters has not found anyone to be in violation of the rules.

The report comes again during the fall semester, and because Ralph is so busy he puts it on his desk for later review. A few weeks go by and the report has still not been reviewed. No one would know that Ralph has not reviewed the report unless someone was found to be in violation of the rules. John is the vice president of the house and works closely with Ralph during busy times. One day while John is looking for something on Ralph's desk, he comes across the report and sees that one of the members of the house has a 2.1 GPA and is carrying only fourteen credits. Puzzled as to why Ralph has not said anything, John looks closely at the report and sees that the member is Roman. If they were to report Roman he would instantly lose his scholarship and have to move out of the house. John wonders, "How could this be happening?"

- What are the issues in this case?
- What are John's options for handling the situation? How might each option play out? Which option do you prefer?
- What do you think John should do? What do you think Ralph should do?
- How should they approach Roman? Should Roman be allowed to stay because he is such a good housemate and works hard for the house? Should he be given a probationary period to get his grades and credit load up?

- What ethical and legal responsibilities do Ralph and John have to the Bass family?

# Unknown Pregnancy

Katie is a senior RA on an all-female floor of a high-rise residence hall. She has forty residents living on her floor in suite-style rooms with four women to a room. They are primarily freshmen, but there are a few sophomores too. The women have developed close personal relationships with one another and building community has never been an issue. The women tend to keep their doors open, are respectful of one another, and tend to follow most rules and community standards.

On Tuesday, Sandy comes to Katie's room upset and anxious about something and tells her that she needs to talk. She tells Katie that she has been feeling nauseous on a daily basis and believes she may be pregnant. Katie asks Sandy if she has been having her period on a monthly basis and she says yes. Katie then tells her that it is not likely that she is pregnant because she has not missed her period. The two of them talk some more and Katie tells Sandy about the counseling center and the health center. Sandy promises that she will make an appointment with the health center to have a pregnancy test done and any other tests that may help explain the nausea. Katie gives Sandy some laxatives, because Katie thinks that may help. Sandy takes two tablets, as the package indicates. It's 2:30 P.M. and Katie has a class to go to, so she tells Sandy that she has to leave and Sandy goes back to her room. At 3:00 Sandy goes up to her loft to get some rest. At 3:30 she feels the urge to go to the bathroom, so she comes down from the loft. She lies down on a throw rug in the middle of the floor in wrenching pain. At 4:00 Katie returns to the hall and decides to check up on Sandy. As she approaches Sandy's room, she hears screaming from inside. When Sandy does not respond to Katie's request to open the door, Katie unlocks the door and enters the room. She finds Sandy lying in a ball on the floor holding her stomach and screaming in pain. Sandy indicates that something horrible is happening to her and at 4:10 she gives birth. Katie instantly calls 911, and at 4:30 the paramedics arrive and take the baby on one gurney and Sandy on another. Katie follows them downstairs to make sure they get to the ambulance without incident. As she arrives at the front desk, Tom, who is working the desk, says that someone from 52 Action News is on the line asking where the student and baby have been taken. Katie grabs the phone and calmly as possible tells this person that she has no knowledge of any student having a baby. After hanging up the phone, she decides to address this situation with the women on her floor because they all know Sandy and will be concerned. She pulls together a floor meeting and explains to them what has happened and does any necessary damage control.

- What are the issues in this case?
- What are Katie's options for handling the situation? How might each option play out? Which option do you prefer?
- How should Katie address this situation with her female residents? How much information should she give them?
- What other offices on campus should be involved in helping Katie and her residents process this situation?
- How do you think Katie handled the situation? Is there something she should have done differently?

## Distribution in the Residence Halls

As the RA on duty, following a routine walk of your residence hall one evening, you realize that it smells like marijuana on the fourth floor. You approach the room where the smell appears to be originating. As you get closer, you realize that many students may be in the room and feel that you should call a fellow RA for backup. After you knock on the door, one student answers not noticing that the student behind him has a joint lit up. It quickly becomes apparent that all of the students in the room are smoking marijuana.

After you call public safety and all the students are arrested, you are called to the resident directors' office with the other RAs in the building. The resident director (RD) says that not only were five students arrested and charged with possession of marijuana but the residents of the room were charged with distributing an illegal drug after twelve marijuana plants were found growing in the room. The RD then goes on to say that the two students charged with distributing said in a confession that at least three RAs in your building and four to five RAs in another building are regular customers for marijuana. The students have not given names but said that they would be willing to identify the RAs in a lineup. You decide to give the RAs an opportunity to turn themselves in now for some reduced penalties at the university. The university does not have a written zero-tolerance policy for possession and use of illegal substances.

- What are the issues in this case?
- What are your options for handling the situation? How might each option play out? Which option do you prefer?
- If the RAs come forward, what penalties and sanctions would they face at the university? How different are these for a student not employed by the university?
- How would you use this situation to look at the university's drug policy? Would you approach this from a residence life perspective or a broad-based university-wide policy?
- Who would be part of the conversations addressing drug use? How would training take place for individuals who may work in situations in which this is a concern?

## Breaking a Rule or a Mere Technicality?

At Orono College, as a staff member of residence life, if you drink alcohol with the residents on your floor, it is a violation of residence life rules. Ruth and Doug are both RAs on the fourth floor of their residence hall, Ruth on the female side and Doug on the male side. Most of the residents living in the hall are juniors and seniors and are of legal age to drink. RAs move in three weeks before the general population for training and to get the hall ready for the fall.

A week before school begins, Ruth and Doug decide to have a party in Ruth's apartment. They decide to make it a small party, just an intimate get-together before the big rush and craziness of the semester begins. They both invite a few of their friends, and ten people, including themselves, are in attendance.

John, the lead RA in the hall, is bored and decides to see what the others are doing. He knocks on Doug's door and gets no answer. He goes down to the B side and finds Ruth's door open and the ten occupants sitting around drinking. He is a bit shocked because some of the students in attendance are the hall's floor residents. He decides not to say anything that night and leaves. The next day John calls both Ruth and Doug into his office to discuss the situation. He reminds them of the rules. Both Ruth and Doug say that they were not doing anything wrong because technically the students will not be residents for another week.

- What are the issues in this case?
- What are John's options for handling the situation? How might each option play out? Which option do you prefer?
- Should Ruth and Doug be written up for a rule violation?
- Are Ruth and Doug using a technicality to break a rule? Or do you feel that Ruth and Doug did not really break any rules?

## Registered Sex Offender Living in Residence

Darlene is a junior RA in Sun Hall at Johnson University. This is her second year as an RA, and she really enjoys her residents and work with residence life. During a campus tour with a group of prospective freshman students and parents, she passes by a room with two male senior students playing video games. She pops her head in and asks if her group can look in and see what a typical residence hall room looks like. The men say that that's fine. As the group is peeking in, one of the mothers in the group gets very upset and along with her daughter runs from the group. Darlene is not quite sure what to do. She takes the group to the lounge and searches for the mother and daughter. She finds them in the bathroom crying hysterically. She asks if something has happened and how she can help. The mother says that one of the men in the room raped her daughter when she was twelve and he was sixteen. She goes on to say that the young man was arrested and is now a registered sex offender living among the students. She demands to see the university president and says she is going to have the young man kicked out of the university because he does not deserve to get an education.

- What are the issues in this case?
- What are Darlene's options for handling the situation? How might each option play out? Which option do you prefer?
- Do other students deserve to know that this student is a registered sex offender?

## HALL COUNCIL ISSUES

## Almost a No-Show

You are the president of the hall council for one of the residential colleges on campus. The residential college houses freshmen through seniors who are all engineering majors. You are excited about a new program for your hall. Once a month, the hall council will provide dinner and a faculty member will discuss potential career opportunities in the engineering field. You decided to offer these programs because the survey you conducted among the residents indicated that they wanted more information on career options. A week before the event, you ask students to sign up to attend because you need to know how much pizza to buy. You are very excited because thirty students signed up. The event is Tuesday at 6:00 P.M. It is 6:01 and the faculty member is present, the pizza is delivered, and only two students have shown up, including yourself.

- What are the issues in this case?
- What are your options for handling the situation? How might each option play out? Which option do you prefer?
- How should you respond? Should you wait a few more minutes to see if anyone else attends? Should you cancel the event if you only have three people? Is there anything you can do to solicit more participation?
- What have you learned from this experience? What should you do next time to ensure better participation? Should you get the rest of your council involved? The residence life staff? Should you provide

reminder e-mails or phone calls? To what lengths should you go to get people to the program?

- How should you handle yourself with the faculty member? Remember that this is the first program in a series and the faculty member may go back and talk to his or her colleagues.

## Where Did They Go?

Sixty people attend your first hall-government meeting. You facilitate a series of icebreakers. Then the executive board is elected, and you discuss goals for the semester, members' expectations, and ways to get involved in the organization. As the president of hall government, you feel pretty good about the first meeting and about the executive appointments. You convene the group the following week and thirty general members attend. You effectively run the meeting by facilitating more icebreakers, allowing each executive officer to share his or her items, discussing new and old business, and then adjourning. The following week you hold another meeting and only ten general members attend. You follow the same agenda as the previous week: brief icebreakers followed by reports and new and old business. You remind the general members of ways in which they can get involved and encourage the executive officers to also get general members involved. The executive officers agree to try but they are a little overwhelmed. They are still figuring out their positions and are not really sure what they are doing, let alone how to include others. The following week you hold the fourth hall-government meeting and only the executive board and two general members attend.

- What are the issues in this case?
- What are your options for handling the situation? How might each option play out? Which option do you prefer?
- Where did your general members go? Why did they stop attending your meetings?
- How should you address this situation? Do you want involvement beyond the executive board? If your executive board is active and enthusiastic, do you need general members? What benefits, if any, do general board members bring to your organization?

- How can you get more people to attend your meetings? What will motivate people to get involved? How might you include them so that they will feel like they are part of your organization?
- Can you turn to your advisor for guidance? Other hall-government presidents? Should you consider requiring more floor representatives?

## Should She Stay or Should She Go?

You are the president of your hall council. Your treasurer, Alexis, is an accounting major and a very dedicated member of the hall council. She handles all the money for the organization and also helps coordinate many of the events. She is one of the best contributors to the organization. Late Friday night, Alexis and Elizabeth, one of the desk workers in the building, come back from a party intoxicated. They start tearing posters and bulletin board decorations off the walls, yelling loudly, and doing cartwheels down the hall. The RA on duty confronts them and writes them up. Their actions are in violation of school policy and they will go through the conduct system. The hall director informs you of Alexis's behavior.

- What are the issues in this case?
- What are your options for handling the situation? How might each option play out? Which option do you prefer?
- Do you think Alexis should remain hall council treasurer or be asked to step down? What should you do if the hall director insists that Alexis be removed from her position?

## Abusing the Privilege?

Joe is a second-year RA. Over the winter break he remains on campus. He is very bored and most of his residents went home for the break. One of his residents, Brett, has many DVDs and video games. During the school year, Brett regularly loans his items to the residents on the floor. Joe decides to key into Brett's room to borrow some of these items to alleviate his boredom.

- What do you think about Joe's actions?
- Is it ever okay to key into a room without the resident's permission?
- If Brett had told Joe that he could borrow anything he wanted over the break, would it be okay for Joe to key into his room? What should happen if Joe agreed, frequently keyed in, and then when Brett returned something was broken or stolen?
- What are your options for handling Joe's behavior?


# How Hard Do I Push?

You are the president of your hall council and one of your executive board members is pregnant. She tells the group and everyone seems to be supportive. As her pregnancy progresses, she starts to slack on her executive board responsibilities. You are hesitant to confront her. You worry that you might come off as insensitive. She might get angry and other members of the executive board might criticize you.

- What are the issues in this case?
- What are your options for handling the situation? How might each option play out? Which option do you prefer?
- Should you treat the board member any differently because she is pregnant?


# You Like Them More Than Us!

The advisor of the residence hall council is also the hall director who supervisors the RAs in your building. She is very tight with money and encourages the hall council to be very conservative with its money. Despite this advice, she is always very eager to allocate the hall-government money to support RA programming. Your group is getting frustrated because she scrutinizes every penny spent by the hall council on programming, yet she gives the RAs anything they want.

- What are the issues in this case?
- What are your options for handling the situation? How might each option play out? Which options do you prefer?
- What should you do if you confront your hall director and she gets angry?

# 4

# STUDENT GOVERNMENT CASES

## Crossing the Political Line

Deb is the president of the student government at Nano College. Nano is a small liberal arts college in a conservative town. The students and faculty at Nano tend to be a bit more liberal than the town and college administration; this often causes tension at all levels. During a recent U.S. presidential election, the student government decides to hold voter registration drives across campus. As a group, the student government decides to make the drives free of any affiliation with a particular political party, candidate, or any other ballot issue.

Deb signs up to work three drives and decides that bringing a few flyers about an antiabortion candidate will be fine; after all, Nano sits in a conservative town with a history of voting for antiabortion candidates. The drives run without incident and students come in large numbers to get registered. Three weeks later at a student government meeting, John, the vice president, brings the student newspaper. On the front page is a picture of Deb handing out the flyers that she brought to the drives. The headline reads, "Voter Registration Drive Urges Student Government to Endorse Pro-life Candidate." John says to Deb, "The executive board of the student government decided to meet without you to discuss this situation. We feel that handing out those flyers at our event was a blatant attempt at promoting one candidate and using the student government to promote your own political agenda." Deb storms out of the room saying, "You cannot hold secret meetings without me. I am the leader of this organization, and I am going to talk with the dean."

- What are the issues in this case?
- What are Deb's options for handling the situation? How might each option play out? Which option do you prefer?
- How should John and the other members of the student government proceed?
- Who in the administration should be consulted?

# What a Site

As the manager of a computer lab on campus, your role is to sign all students in and out of the lab, make sure printers are filled with paper, and monitor the general behavior in the lab. Because it is a study space for many students, you need to make sure that it is quiet and that students are respectful of one another. Being the manager of the lab is your work-study position, and this job allows you to have enough money to finance part of your education and also be involved with on-campus groups. Your real passion is your involvement with the student government. You are the president elect and are very excited about your upcoming presidential year. You have some great ideas and are working with an excellent current president, who you feel has been a great mentor.

One night while working in the lab, the president of the student government signs in to use the lab. You chat for a bit and he goes to a computer and works for about two hours. At the end of your shift, which is also closing time for the lab, you have to make sure all the computers are powered down, the screens turned off, and chairs pushed in. Many students forget to power down their computers and some even forget to log out. As you get to the second row of computers, you find that many screens are still displaying the site that the user was visiting. You have a hard time believing that your fellow classmates cannot turn off their computers and push in their chairs when they are finished working. "How hard is that?" you think.

As you shut down one of the computers, an extremely graphic picture pops up on the screen. Stunned, you think, "Who was looking at this pornographic site?" You check the log-in book and find that the president of the student government was using that computer and that he was the last one to use it. Using the campus network and computers to look at pornographic sites is a violation and can result in expulsion from the school. What should you do?

- What are the issues in this case?
- What are your options for handling the situation? How might each option play out? Which option do you prefer?
- How would you proceed if you were the computer lab student manager?
- What responsibilities does the computer lab manager have in this case? Are they different because she has an additional role as the president elect of the student government?
- How should the president of the student government be treated? Does it matter that he is a campus leader?

## Big Trouble in Paradise

The campus of Waikiki University (WU) has always been referred to as paradise for most islanders and prospective students. The landscaping and views from most academic and residential buildings are breathtaking. At WU the student government is very strong and involved in many decisions on campus. Ana is the senior president, Keoni is the senior vice president, and Kala and Kawe are the two sophomore-class representatives.

The administration at WU has decided to close the on-campus bar. Sony Bar has been in the basement of the student union for many years and has become a landmark on campus. Students are allowed in the bar only if they are of legal drinking age, and the bar is only open Thursday, Friday, and Saturday nights. The administration at WU has met with the board of regents, and the decision to close the bar was finalized with no input from the student government or student body. Ana is not upset about the bar's closing but is sure that the student government will hear many complaints; this incident will confirm for many that the role of the student government is advisory with no authority.

Ana calls a meeting of the student government executive board members. Kawe says to the board, "Who do they think pays tuition and fees at this school?" Keoni adds, "They should not be allowed to keep making policy decisions with little or no input from the student body." Ana chimes in,

"At least they did not say they asked us for input. It was a closed-door meeting and we did not have a representative present." Kala remarks, "That's good because I don't want to have to take a bunch of flack from the students. My housemates love the Sony and it has done well for the school. Not one incident has happened since the place opened, and students have always had fun." As the meeting concludes, Ana says, "It will be interesting to see how this all plays out."

The next day, in the community newspaper, an article about Sony Bar is on the front page. It reads, "Based on feedback from the student body and community members, the decision was made to close Sony Bar." It goes on to quote the school president, Dr. Lopeka, as saying, "The university community has made this decision based on many conversations and surveys of the affected constituents. We feel that promoting an institution that serves alcohol is not in the best interest of WU. We are closing the Sony to open a new coffee shop for everyone in the community. We hope to bring not only the WU family together, but also local residents."

Outraged, Ana immediately calls Keoni and says, "How can they just misrepresent us like that? They never talked to us or the student body once. I am done; I have had enough of this crap. I am going to call Dean Buggler today and resign." Keoni replies, "Hold on, Ana. Let's think this through and talk with Dean Buggler and see if we can get an appointment with Dr. Lopeka," replies Keoni. "Go ahead. I am done!" screams Ana and hangs up the phone.

- What are the issues in this case?
- What are the options for handling the situation? How might each option play out? Which option do you prefer?

## Unclear Boundaries

Maria's role on the student government is to serve as the liaison for student organizations. Early into the semester, it becomes evident that the boundaries of her position are unclear. For example, the vice president of student government sends a welcome letter to all student organizations on behalf of the government. This confuses and upsets Maria because she thinks that is her job. She also worries that others will think she isn't doing her job. When she asks the vice president why he sent the letter, he tells her that he thought it was his job and that he has no intention of stepping on her toes.

- What are the issues in this case?
- What are Maria's options for handling the situation? How might each option play out? Which option do you prefer?
- A breakdown in communication seems to be the root of this problem. What would you suggest that the organization do to prevent future miscommunications?
- How does your organization distribute the workload? Do you have clear job descriptions for each officer? Do you regularly discuss the responsibilities of each member? Are new officers trained by outgoing officers? How might your organization improve in this area?

## Those Freshmen

Kolvaris College is a small, private religiously affiliated college in the South. During its first month of the beginning semester at Kolvaris, the freshman class has had more incidents of alcohol abuse than any of the previous ten incoming classes. Six weeks into the school year, the administration decides to impose a new policy that any underage student who is caught consuming alcohol will suffer serious consequences including social probation. Social probation prohibits students from studying abroad and from joining a sorority or fraternity. These are grave consequences, given that more than half of the students at Kolvaris study abroad, and that more than half are members of the Greek system. In addition to social probation, the administration will send parents a letter notifying them of their child's misconduct.

Janine is the president of the student government association. Many members of the student government are upset by the administration's reaction. The members of the student government who are extremely upset decide to hold a town hall meeting to listen to students' concerns and accept suggested revisions to current policy. At this meeting, the group writes a new resolution with alternatives to the policy. The members suggest that first offenses will result in a written warning, a twenty-five-dollar fine, and attendance at an alcohol education seminar. Second offenses will result in social probation, and third offenses will involve a letter to parents. Janine presents this alternative to the president, who denies the request without explanation. The students are upset and believe that their voices are not being heard. They continue to debate the issue in the school newspaper throughout the academic year. Once summer arrives, the students go home, and interest in the drinking policy dies. In the fall, a new freshman class attends Kolvaris, but the new students don't question the policy, because to them this is a firm policy and there is no need to question an established rule.

- What are the issues in this case?
- What are Janine and the student government association's options for handling the situation? How might each option play out? Which option do you prefer?
- Why do you think the issue died? Have you ever been passionate about an idea and then watched people lose interest toward the end of the school year? How do you determine which battles to fight? How hard and how long do you fight them?
- What do you think of the president's response to the students' request? What are some options for the students to get more feedback on their proposal? Have you ever felt like student voices were not heard by the administration? How did you handle this problem?

## Smoking, Anyone?

One of the important agenda items for your presidency is the implementation of a no-smoking policy in all the residence halls. When you approach the vice president for student affairs about your ambitious idea, she suggests that you need to exhibit student support. Following this advice, the student government launches a phone survey to poll student opinions of this topic. Your group randomly surveys the campus via telephone. Your records indicate that you connect with 25 percent of the student body and that 85 percent support the smoking ban. As a result, you write an initial resolution for three of the twenty residence halls to become smoke free. The legislation quickly passes through the student government but is then vetoed by the administration. The administration explains that the veto was necessary because no one informed admissions. Members of the admissions staff were unaware of this initiative and had promised prospective students that they could smoke in the halls next year.

- What are the issues in this case?
- What are your options for handling the problem? How might each option play out? Which option do you prefer?
- In your opinion, where was the breakdown in communication? How might you prevent future communication errors?
- When your organization begins new initiatives, do you discuss the potential stakeholders? Do you think about who needs to be informed? How might doing this have helped in this situation? Do you ever make decisions without informing other constituents? How can this potentially impede the progress of your organization?
- Is this idea dead? How might the student government implement it in the future? Is there any compromise that might be made?

## Recycling on Campus

Dan is the president of the student government at Yishane University. As an environmental biology major, he is extremely passionate about and committed to recycling on campus. Currently, Yishane University does not have a recycling program on campus and Dan is not sure why. At the next student government meeting, he brings up this issue during the discussion of new business. Most of the students are supportive and don't understand why the school doesn't already have a program; after all, Yishane University has an excellent reputation for its engineering, architecture, and natural-science programs. The group discusses the issue and decides that Dan, as president, can do some fact finding and share his findings with the group at next month's meeting.

Dan begins his fact-finding quest by talking with individuals in the facilities department. This office is responsible for waste removal on campus and would be the office to run the recycling program. Marty, the director, is receptive to the idea but feels that his budget cannot accommodate the extra expense that this program would require. Next Dan decides to talk with Lisa, the dean of students, and Tammy, the director of residence life. Lisa is the advisor for the student government and a huge fan of Dan's. Dan feels that he will get support from Lisa and also Tammy, who was his supervisor for two years and with whom he feels he has a good relationship. He finds both women extremely receptive to the program, but they are unable to provide the funding and support to get the program up and running.

Frustrated and not sure where else to go, Dan decides to talk with Sateesh, an advanced graduate student in biology who is well connected outside the university. Sateesh has done many internships with environmental groups and governmental agencies during his academic tenure. He tells Dan about a group called Sierra Recycling that comes to campuses across the country to help them start recycling programs with little or no cost. Dan is very excited and asks Sateesh, "How can I get in touch with this group?" Sateesh says, "Well, there is something you need to know. The group is under suspicion of using a company that is known to violate child labor laws in the production of its T-shirts and other clothing." Dan then asks, "How public and reliable is this information?" Sateesh replies, "It is very well known and many other campuses will not use the company because of the investigation. It was uncovered four years ago and has never been proven either way. The company has not made a comment either way. It seems to ignore this cloud over its head." Sateesh also goes on to tell Dan about seven other companies that provide the same services to campuses, but cost a lot more to the universities. Dan is not sure what to do and it seems that Sierra Recycling may be the only option for Yishane to have a program.

- What are the issues in this case?
- What are Dan's options for handling the situation? How might each option play out? Which option do you prefer?
- Does Dan have an obligation to tell the student government about his knowledge of the company?
- Should the cloud of suspicion that Sierra Recycling is facing be a factor in the decision-making process at Yishane University?
- How important is this information to the university as a whole?

# When to Tell

Officers of the student government association are often privy to information that hasn't been disseminated to the general student body. For example, the president of Ridel College informs the student government president, Leilani, that he wants to change the focus of one of the cooperative-living communities. According to the president, the co-op of women's studies majors is not working. There are not enough women to fill the building and they are not generating enough income to offset the cost of their living expenses. At the beginning of the fall semester, the president informs Leilani that he plans to change the co-op into a Christian co-op. At the beginning of the second semester, the president still hasn't informed the members of the co-op. Leilani knows members of the co-op and feels obligated to tell them that they need to increase their capacity or else risk losing their living arrangements for next year.

- What are the issues in this case?
- What are Leilani's options for handling the situation? How might each option play out? Which option do you prefer?
- Should Leilani make it her responsibility to tell the members of the co-op? Should the members of the co-op be given the chance to improve their numbers and make a profit? What right do the members of the co-op have?
- If the president asks Leilani not to tell the members of the co-op, what should she do? Should the president be allowed to make the change over the summer when the students aren't around?
- Have you ever been in a position as a student leader when you were privy to confidential information? Did you share the secrets? Why or why not? When would you ever break a confidence?

# Rookie President

Yao, a student government president, was elected as a junior despite the fact that he has never served in student government before. Although Yao is a born charismatic leader who has great potential to lead the organization, about half the government officers and senators are eager to see him fail. In the first semester, this dissenting group votes down any legislation that Yao supports. It quickly becomes apparent that Sheila, the government's secretary, does not appreciate him and is one of the ringleaders of the unsupportive group. Not knowing that she would be such a troublemaker, Yao had actually appointed her to the secretarial position because she held the same role the previous year. Although Sheila is a nonvoting member of government and does not speak in general meetings, during executive board meetings she is very vocal and speaks in opposition to Yao. Her position is a paid one, and she is slow to get the minutes out and to perform other aspects of her secretarial responsibilities. Discouraged by her attitude and lack of follow-through, Yao sits down with Sheila to give her feedback on her performance. He also develops an action plan with an appropriate time frame for her to improve. Sheila becomes irate. She believes that he has criticized her performance as a secretary because she does not support his opinions. She does not change her behavior or her work performance.

- What are the issues in this case?
- What are Yao's options for handling the situation? How might each option play out? Which option do you prefer? Does the fact that Sheila is paid impact your decision?
- How do you think firing Sheila would impact the rest of the organization? If this is your preference, how should Yao inform the group?
- Do you have any suggestions for how Yao might turn his nonsupporters into supporters?

## Fiscal Responsibility

Reza is the new student government president. Early in her first semester, the new treasurer comes to Reza and points out some discrepancies in last year's accounting. He cannot account for approximately $10,000. Because all checks require two signatures, he is convinced that the money was embezzled by the previous treasurer and president, who have now graduated. There are receipts for purchases of electronic equipment and furniture, but this equipment and furniture cannot be found.

- What are the issues in this case?
- What are Reza's options for handling the situation? How might each option play out? Which option do you prefer?
- If after further investigation it is proven that the two former officers did embezzle the money, what should be done? Who needs to be informed and involved? Is there any way to get the money back? Should Reza even try?
- What are your current accounting practices? What are your checks and balances procedures for ensuring the proper spending of student government money? How involved is your advisor in ensuring the financial well-being of your organization?
- Do you discuss appropriate spending in your meetings? How do members know what they can and cannot buy on behalf of the organization?

## Compensation for the President and Vice President

Manuel is the president of the student body. He's done his research. At campuses similar in size and mission to his own, the student government president and vice president receive free tuition, in the form of a scholarship, for their year in office. Manuel makes one of his goals for his term to be the tuition waiver for future presidents and vice presidents. He presents his idea and his research findings to the rest of the members of the student government and they seem to think it is an idea worth pursuing. The student newspaper catches wind of the free tuition idea and blasts Manuel. It calls the proposal unnecessary and selfish. Manuel feels it is important to pursue the tuition waiver because it sends a message that the university values student leaders. Additionally, Manuel does not believe that he is acting selfishly because he is advocating that these new scholarships be implemented for his successors and he will not personally benefit if the scholarships are awarded.

- What are the issues in this case?
- What are Manuel's options for handling the situation? How might each option play out? Which option do you prefer?

- Why do you think the school newspaper took such a negative approach to this idea? How might Manuel better communicate his agenda with key members of this publication?
- What is your relationship with the members of your school's newspaper like? How are your ideas communicated? Could you benefit from a better working relationship? How might you improve the current relationship?
- Have you ever been at odds with the school newspaper? How did you handle that situation?

## Loss of a Testing Center

Due to budget cuts, a university president elects to shut down the student testing center. This becomes an important issue among the members of the student body. They want the testing center reopened because there is no alternative location for testing. This impacts students with disabilities, students needing to take make-up exams, and other students with extenuating circumstances. Sasha, the student body president, does not personally share the sentiments of the rest of the students. She understands why the president had to make this tough decision and also knows that the student disability office can be used to test students with disabilities. Additionally, faculty can work additional hours to help facilitate make-up exams or other special needs. Sasha feels torn. Although she supports the president's decision, she also knows that it is her responsibility to represent the students. The students demand that the testing center reopen, and Sasha believes that she must advocate the desires of her constituents. She schedules a meeting with the president and forms a committee to examine the need for a testing center on campus.

- What are the issues in this case?
- What are Sasha's options for handling the situation? How might each option play out? Which option do you prefer?
- Whom does Sasha represent? Does she represent herself and her own interests or does she represent the students? If she is more informed than the general student body, should she then advocate her own opinion if she believes it is in the best interest of the students?

- Have you ever shared your own opinion rather than that of the students you represent? Why? How did that make you feel?
- Have you ever had to advocate for something that you didn't personally believe in? If so, why?

# The Lone Voice

Student government president Amal is often the only student voice in a room full of administrators who think they know what students want or what is best for the students. This is the case on the strategic planning committee, the search committee for the new provost, the planning and development committee, and the budget allocation committee. Amal's personal opinion is that most administrators do not have a clue about what students want. For example, when the administrative planning committee is designing the new student union, Amal advocates for a new wireless coffeehouse with lots of overstuffed chairs, warm colors, and coffee available in a great variety of flavors. She tries to explain to the planning committee that students need a place to hang out late into the night because currently there is no alternative on campus. However, other members of the committee quickly dismiss her idea.

- What are the issues in this case?
- What are Amal's options for handling the situation? How might each option play out? Which option do you prefer?
- Have you ever been in a situation in which you were the lone student voice? How did you advocate for the needs of students? How did you make your voice heard?
- How do you currently assess the needs and wants of students? How might Amal better advocate for the needs of students?

# Raising the Student Activity Fee

The student government association wants to increase the campus activity fee. The current fee has not increased in the past ten years although the amount requested from student organizations continues to increase each year. Karim, a member of the student government, makes it his personal agenda to see that the increase is passed in the upcoming election. He works hard to push it through. He lobbies many student organizations by promising them that they will get a lot of money. He also creates a campus survey to assess student support but asks very leading questions such as, "Would you like more money for student programming?" What he fails to ask is whether or not students are willing to pay an extra hundred dollars per year to support the increase in funds. Based on positive responses from the skewed survey, the student government puts the item on the ballot. Karim words the ballot questions and, again, his questions are misleading. The ballot reads, "Do you want more programming money available on campus? How much should the university allot for programming?" The ballot does not state how much the fee will increase. Although the rest of the student government knows that the ballot questions are misleading, they desperately need the increase to pass.

- What are the issues in this case?
- What are the options for handling the situation? How might each option play out? Which option do you prefer?
- What do you think about Karim's actions? What do you think about the misleading ballot questions? How might the members of the student government rephrase the ballot? Should they inform students of the increase even though they know that the students will probably vote no?
- What are some more honest strategies for advocating for the increase? Should these be implemented or is what Karim and the student government did okay?

## Elections Fiasco

Eva is a first-year graduate student. During the end of her first year, she decides to run for president of the student government. The bylaws of the student government state that students have to have minimum GPA to run. However, because Eva is in her first semester, she doesn't have a GPA yet. A major debate ensues among the members of the student government. Some want to make her eligible by using her undergraduate grades. Others want to hold firm to the policy and believe that first-semester students, undergraduate or graduate, should not be allowed to run. One option that they consider is to let Eva run and if she wins she must meet the GPA requirement. This means that she must meet the GPA requirement before assuming office. Ben, the elections chair, makes an executive decision and tells Eva that she can run. The next day, he meets with the members of the election committee. They are very angry with his decision, because he did not consult with them, and they insist that he reverse his decision. Ben tells Eva that she is no longer eligible. Eva immediately informs Kyle, the student government president, of the situation. Kyle is outraged by the lack of consistency and is extremely frustrated with Ben's unprofessional behavior and lack of leadership. He isn't sure if he should remove Ben from his position or continue with the election. If he removes Ben, there is a chance that he will enter his name in the presidential election. According to the bylaws, if the president removes the election chair from office, then the election chair is eligible to run for president. Kyle is not in favor of Ben becoming the new president of student government.

- What are the issues in this case?
- What are the options for handling the situation? How might each option play out? Which option do you prefer?
- What do you think of Ben's leadership? If his incompetence was intentional so that he could run for president, should this influence Kyle's decision?
- Should Kyle's personal opinion of Ben factor into the decision in any way?
- What is the right thing to do for Eva?

# The Stalker

Dmitri is the president of the student government. Otto is one of the student senators. Otto enjoys a good debate and likes to argue. He often disagrees with most student government initiatives. He tends to vote against each new piece of legislation, and most members perceive him as a negative entity. During government meetings, he takes the floor and doesn't give it up; he ignores time limits. Recently, on at least three occasions, Otto waits for Dmitri outside his office so that he can promote his agenda. Dmitri is starting to feel harassed, even stalked.

- What are the issues in this case?
- What are Dmitri's options for handling the situation? How might each option play out? Which option do you prefer?
- Should Dmitri be concerned with Otto's behavior? What should he do if Otto threatens physical harm?
- Have you ever had an overzealous member in your organization? How did you handle the situation?

## Dematriculated Executive Board Member

Kalani is a member of the executive board of student government. Unfortunately, he did not meet the minimum GPA to continue in his position. Actually, his grades were so bad that he was dematriculated from the university but didn't tell anyone. He continues to keep this secret so that he can keep his membership in the student government. He is extremely involved and committed to the organization.

Part of the secretary's responsibility is to confirm all members' GPAs and enrollment status each semester. Scott, one of Kalani's friends and fellow executive board members, is aware of Kalani's academic status. He keeps hinting to the secretary that she should run the enrollment checks, but it is now the fourth week of the semester and the check hasn't even been started. Scott is torn about what to do. Kalani is a very dedicated student leader. He volunteers for committees and does a good job. In fact, the student government is so important to Kalani that it is the only thing keeping him going right now.

- What are the issues in this case?
- What are Scott's options for handling the situation? How might each option play out? Which option do you prefer?
- Do you know of students who are so involved in their leadership organizations that they let their grades slip? What does your organization

do to promote academics? How do you encourage the proper balance between involvement and academics?

## To Remove a Chair or Not to Remove a Chair

Gabriel is the vice president in charge of committees. During the first semester, he doesn't see much action from the committee chairs. Despite his ongoing feedback to them, he sees little improvement. He is now debating the replacement of five of the ten committee chairs. However, he discovers that one of the ineffective chairs, Stacy, plans to run for president of the student government in the spring. Gabriel plans to run as well. As a result, Gabriel is hesitant to remove Stacy from her committee chair position because people will believe that it is an election ploy.

- What are the issues in this case?
- What are Gabriel's options for handling the situation? How might each option play out? Which option do you prefer?
- Because Gabriel wants to be president next year, what is the best alternative? Should his priority be to have the most effective committees during this academic year? How do you weigh his personal motivations in your decision-making process?
- Should Gabriel keep Stacy in her current role but then discuss her ineffectiveness behind her back? What would be the pros and cons of doing so? Do you know organizational leaders who gossip behind each other's backs? How do you handle the situation?

## The Charismatic Vice President

Hasan is the president of student government. Joseph, the vice president, is Hasan's best friend. Joseph is very charismatic and well known and well liked on campus. Many feel that Hasan was elected president because of his running mate's popularity. Hasan asked Joseph to run as his vice president because he trusts him as a friend. He recognizes Joseph's shortcomings as vice president. For example, Joseph has never run a meeting and doesn't understand parliamentary procedure. Many senators believe that his meetings are unprofessional. He plays music at the start of meetings and likes to order pizza and do icebreakers. He's been criticized for wasting time with these activities. People, especially experienced government members who have "real agendas" for the meetings, get frustrated and often leave. This often means that Joseph loses quorum before starting the agenda.

Although Joseph has never been involved in student government, he is a leader on campus. He is a resident assistant, which opens him up to critical comments by experienced government members such as, "This is student government, not the Residence Hall Association." Shortly into Joseph's term, he resigns. Some speculate that Joseph resigned because he ran with Hasan only to help him be elected president and that he never intended to assume the responsibility of his position as vice president. However, Hasan knows that Joseph resigned because he didn't appreciate all the criticism.

- What are the issues in this case?
- What are Hasan's options for handling the situation? How might each option play out? Which option do you prefer?
- Is there anything that Hasan or Joseph could have done to respond to the criticism and prevent Joseph's resignation?
- How should Hasan handle the negative fallout from Joseph's resignation?

# 5

# GREEK LIFE CASES

## Same Fraternity/Sorority, Different Rules

Your chapter tends to play by the rules. When hosting social functions, you, the chapter president, have a strict guest list, use a third-party vendor, and have designated drivers. You are invited to attend a chapter function at a neighboring college. Upon arrival, you are shocked to learn that this chapter is nothing like your own. The members are obviously partiers. Alcohol flows freely, no one is carded, and everyone is very intoxicated. When you return to campus, your members start to complain about your strict compliance to the national rules. They do not want to become as out of control as the other chapter; they just want to loosen up a bit. They don't understand why they always have to be the goody-goody chapter.

- What are the issues in this case?
- What are your options for handling the situation? How might each option play out? Which option do you prefer?
- Should you contact the national office to inform it of the neighboring chapter's behavior? Why or why not?

- What will happen if you fail to adhere to the requirements of the fraternity insurance purchasing group (FIPG) regulations and there is an incident in your chapter involving alcohol, such as an underage new member experiencing alcohol poisoning?

## Cocaine, Anyone?

Over the course of the semester, you learn that one of your brothers is regularly using cocaine. Other members of your chapter spotted him buying drugs and then using them at a local party. He has also encouraged other chapter members to try the drug. You know that he regularly smokes marijuana, but a handful of members in your chapter also do and no one says anything.

- What are the issues in this case?
- What are your options for handling the situation? How might each option play out? Which option do you prefer?
- What should you do if the member's drug use escalates to an addiction? What should you do if he does recruit other members to use drugs?
- In deciding whether or not to keep the member in the chapter, do you do what is best for him or what is best for the chapter? Do you think he was thinking of the chapter when he decided to use drugs?
- Would it make a difference if the member was doing drugs in the chapter house? What about in an off-campus apartment?
- What should you do if your chapter starts to get a reputation for having members who use drugs?

## Raise the GPA or Else

Your chapter's overall grade point average (GPA) is 2.67. Although this is above the non-Greek average, it is in the bottom third among the other fraternities/sororities. Your national officer visits and puts the chapter on academic probation. It is expected that you will increase your chapter's GPA to

2.8 within a year. The consultant does not give you any suggestions for increasing the GPA. You currently require a minimum 2.5 GPA to remain in good standing. The first semester that brothers/sisters fall below the minimum, they are given a warning and have to attend mandatory study hours. The second semester, they are placed on social probation. The third semester, they may be released from the chapter. One of the strategies that the executive board decides to implement to meet the national mandate is to increase the minimum GPA from 2.5 to 2.8. Many members become very upset about the change and threaten to disaffiliate from the chapter. They are upset because they were recruited with the 2.5 minimum, and now are going to be kicked out if they don't get a 2.8. They argue that all the other chapters require only a 2.5 as the minimum GPA; if the executive board decides to raise the GPA for new members, this could impact your chapter during recruitment.

- What are the issues in this case?
- What are your options for handling the situation? How might each option play out? Which option do you prefer?
- Do you have any other suggestions for increasing your chapter's GPA?
- Should you consider contacting the national office for its perspective on your chapter's GPA? Do you think it might offer suggestions or clarification regarding the consultant's mandate?

## How Many Members Make an Event?

Four brothers live together in an apartment. They decide to host a St. Patrick's Day party. They announce the party on their various Facebook lists. In their announcements, they mention a keg and recommend that you come early if you are underage. They also extend an open invitation to your chapter but claim that it is not a "chapter" event. About a third of your chapter members attend the party, including most of the new, underage members. The party gets loud and one of the neighbors calls the police. The police break up the party and issue many possession charges to minors, most of whom are members of your chapter.

- What are the issues in this case?
- What are your options for handling the situation? How might each option play out? Which option do you prefer?
- Is this a chapter event? How many members need to be in attendance in order for an event to be considered a chapter function? Is an event a chapter function if it is announced at a chapter meeting? Is it a chapter function if it is put on the chapter e-mail list or Facebook list?
- What should you do if your Greek judicial board learns of the incident and wants to hold your chapter accountable?

## BYOB

Your fraternity hosts a BYOB party with a guest list. One of the guests on the list drinks too much, gets into her car and starts driving home, and then gets into a car wreck. Some of the alcohol that she drank was her own, and some of it was given to her by chapter members. She tells the police that she was drinking at your chapter house. The police come to your chapter house and ask to see the president.

- What are the issues in this case?
- What are your options for handling the situation? How might each option play out? Which option do you prefer?
- What are the necessary components of FIPG that need to be followed when hosting a party? How will your national office support you if you are in compliance? How will it support you if you are not in compliance?
- At what point do you contact your national office?

## Girl Crazy

Your national officer/consultant schedules a three-day visit with your chapter. Upon his arrival, he asks some of the brothers to take him to the local bar. At the bar, he consumes alcohol and hits on many of the women there. The brothers come back to the chapter house and tell everyone about the cool consultant. In the following three days, he meets with chapter members during the day and then hits the bar with them each night.

- What are the issues in this case?
- What are your options for handling the situation? How might each option play out? Which option do you prefer?
- What should you do if the national officer hits on your friends? What should you do if his advances are unwanted and the women find him offensive and inappropriate?
- Should you confront the national officer? Could this impact his evaluation of the chapter? At what point do you notify the national office of the officer's behavior?
- What is the purpose of visits from members of your national office? How might these visits benefit your chapter?

## Who Is Your Big Sister?

During the new-member period, all new members are assigned a big sister. The big sister is typically a member of last year's new-member class. Initially, the pairing is a surprise for the new member. For one week, not knowing who her big sister is, the little sister is showered with gifts and notes by her big sister. At the end of the week, there is a ceremony at which the names of the big sisters are revealed followed by a big-sisterhood event. This is a major tradition for your chapter. Somehow, this year all the new members know the names of their big sisters. The element of surprise is ruined. Some of the big sisters are very angry and go on a "witch hunt" throughout the chapter to find out who revealed their names. Two members confront one big sister, Sam, and accuse her of the act. She denies it and gets very upset by their accusations. They threaten to turn her in to the standards board and warn her that she'd better keep her mouth shut in the future regarding chapter business. As it turns out, Amy, a gossipy new member of another chapter, asked each big sister of your chapter for the name of her little sister. She is the one who told all the little sisters the names of their big sisters before the party.

- What are the issues in this case?
- What are your options for handling the situation? How might each option play out? Which option do you prefer?
- How should you handle the two sisters who threatened Sam? If Sam had revealed the secret, would their actions be justified? What would you do if the two sisters had physically hurt her?
- What should you do if Sam is innocent but the two girls tell the entire chapter that she revealed the secret and now no one will talk to her? What should you do if Sam then wants to quit the chapter?
- What should you do about Amy?
- Is there any way to salvage the big-sister ceremony? How do you handle things within your chapter?

## Sorority Awards

You are Renee, the social chairwoman for the Kappa Phi social sorority at Lakers University. A major part of your responsibility is to organize the spring social. It is a major event for the sorority. It is an opportunity to celebrate the accomplishments of the past academic year, publicly pass the gavel to the new president and leadership team, as well as entertain alumni who are major financial donors to the sorority. Since you were inducted your sophomore year, it has been your dream to be social chair during your senior year. After months of organizing, planning, and coordinating for the event, the night of the event finally arrives.

You arrive at the conference center first and begin putting the finishing touches on table arrangements and conferring with the banquet staff. About a half hour later, the other five members of the planning team arrive and you delegate some final tasks. Judith wants you to take one final look at the mock awards to make sure she has not forgotten anything. The mock awards are a major part of the celebration. There are ten awards that get voted on by the active membership. The awards are a fun part of the evening and have become legendary over the years. Most of the awards are the same each year: best dressed, best hair, biggest flirt, and so forth. You really do not have time to scrutinize the awards. You trust Judith so you give the awards a cursory glance and go back to taking care of the finishing touches.

As the evening progresses, you take a step back and marvel at how everything is really going perfectly. You could not be more proud of yourself. Around 8:00 P.M. it is time to begin the formal program. The program goes smoothly and, finally, it is time for the mock awards. Judith takes the podium and goes through the first few awards with lots of laughter from participants. She says, "And now, for our final mock award of the year—a new one—the award for the Most Ghetto in Kappa Phi goes to Pam Webb." There is an audible gasp in the crowd and no one moves. At the end of the program, you call Judith over and ask, "What was that all about?" Judith says, "We decided to make up this award because Pam tries so hard to be 'ghetto.'" You respond, "What does that mean? Did you think about who this might offend and how it makes the sorority look?" She replies, "Well, we thought it was funny, and I guess we didn't think about those things."

- What are the issues in this case?
- What are your options for handling the situation? How might each option play out? Which option do you prefer?
- What steps should Renee take as the social chair for Kappa Phi?
- What offices and constituencies should Renee and Kappa Phi work with on campus?

## New Initiates Gone Wild

You are in your first semester as chapter president. The standards board typically meets after each chapter meeting. This week, there is a line of sisters waiting to meet with the standards board. All want to discuss two recently initiated members who allegedly sleep around. Members addressing the board claim that these two sisters often get drunk, strip at parties, kiss other girls, openly discuss their sexual escapades, and disclose elements of ritual. The standards board meeting quickly turns into a town hall meeting. Sisters start to cry. Many threaten to deactivate if the women are not released from the chapter. The board members thank the sisters for bringing the situation to their attention. After a lengthy discussion, the board members call in the two recently initiated sisters and release them from the chapter. Later, the big sisters of the two released members burst into the standards board meeting crying and demanding that the two new members be reinstated. The big sisters are two of your best friends. They inform you that the women are positive members of the chapter and that their behaviors are not as extreme as the others made them out to be.

- What are the issues in this case?
- What are your options for handling the situation? How might each option play out? Which option do you prefer?
- Are there any other options for disciplining the new initiates? If the accusations about their behavior are true, what should you do? If the sisters embellished the actions of the initiates, what should you do? Does it make a difference that their advocates are your good friends?
- Can you reverse your decision after you have released someone from the chapter? If so, what message would a reversed decision send to your chapter?
- If the removal holds, how will you face your two friends?

## Live Out

All chapter members are required to live in the chapter house for two semesters. Prior to initiation, all new members sign a statement agreeing to this policy. While they are told that the house must remain full for financial reasons, many believe that living in the house is an opportunity to really get to know their sisters and bond as a chapter. However, despite the benefits of living in the house, some sisters come up with extreme excuses not to live in. Most plead that they cannot afford it; others claim to be mentally unstable. One sister admits to having an eating disorder that prevents her from living in the house; she cannot let people watch her eat. Each plea is compelling, but you know that if you let everyone out of the requirement, you will no longer be able to afford the house.

- What are the issues in this case?
- What are your options for handling the situation? How might each option play out? Which option do you prefer?
- Although all the live-out pleas are moving and appear sincere, where do you draw the line? What happens if you let one person out of the

requirement but not another? Are there some cases that warrant release from the requirement? How do you make exceptions?

- Since release from the housing requirement is an ongoing issue in
your chapter, how do you proactively address it? Is signing the contract prior to initiation working or do you need to do something else?

## Should We Stay or Should We Go?

Your chapter holds a new-member celebration at a local bar. One senior
keeps feeding drinks to an underage new member, Brad. Brad gets very intoxicated and two sober brothers decide to take him home. Rather than take
him to his residence hall room, they take him to the chapter house so they
can keep an eye on him and avoid a possible run-in with the residence life
staff. In the basement of the chapter house, Brad vomits repeatedly, he falls
in and out of consciousness, and his eyes roll back in his head. By this time,
most of the chapter members have returned and are in the basement arguing
about what to do about Brad. About half the members want to take him to
the hospital, but the other half doesn't because they fear the chapter will get
in trouble or that Brad will be charged for underage possession of alcohol.
The chapter president's gut tells him to take Brad to the hospital, but he asks
one brother, who is also a resident assistant (RA), for his assessment. The RA
says that he would have taken Brad to the hospital thirty minutes ago. Despite criticism from half the chapter, the president takes Brad to the hospital,
where the doctors determine that Brad indeed was experiencing alcohol poisoning and could have died if he had not been brought in.

- What are the issues in this case?
- What are your options for handling the situation? How might each
option play out? Which option do you prefer?
- Why did some members put the reputation of the chapter ahead of
the health of a brother? Is Brad's condition "normal" among college
students? When should you suspect that someone has alcohol poisoning? When a brother is intoxicated, should you just let him "sleep it
off"?

- What would have happened if you took Brad to the hospital and found out that he did not have alcohol poisoning? What would have happened if you hadn't taken Brad to the hospital and he died?
- How do you handle this situation with your Greek advisor/university administration or your national office?
- Should you contact Brad's family?

## Recruitment Violations Can Be a Blessing

Your chapter receives a recruitment violation because one of your active members is spotted talking with a prospective member during strict silence period. As a result, your chapter is placed on social probation for one semester. You cannot host, cosponsor, or attend any social functions as a chapter. You are the chapter president and need to break the news to your chapter. Although you know the members will be disappointed, you are excited because the probation means you can now focus the chapter's energies on something other than parties and drinking. You know that your chapter is about more than the alcohol, but you fear that some sisters belong only for the social outlet. This will be a great opportunity to focus on sisterhood, leadership, and philanthropy.

- What are the issues in this case?
- What are your options for handling the situation? How might each option play out? Which option do you prefer?
- How do you convince the chapter to focus on the positive rather than on losing the alcohol?
- What should you do if some chapter members want to take the parties underground, that is, still hold them but make them a secret?
- Is your chapter all about the parties or is it about more than that?
- What are some alternatives to the parties?

## I Heard He's a Great Guy

Your chapter is trying to decide whether it should extend a bid to a new transfer student. Your chapter members typically don't extend bids until they have known a student for a semester, but one of the sororities recommended him, as did a few of the brothers. A heated debate ensues.

- What are the issues in this case?
- What are your options for handling the situation? How might each option play out? Which option do you prefer?
- What would happen if you extend the new transfer student a bid and he turns out to be a big partyer and womanizer? What would happen if you extend the bid and he turns out to be a good guy?
- What risk is involved in extending a bid to a person you barely know? How many new members have you chosen not to initiate? Do you have any active members you wish you hadn't initiated?

## Sleep Over

You are a junior and the social chair of your sorority chapter. The annual spring formal is held at a nice hotel. Buses transport the chapter members and their dates. This year, a group of seniors decide that they want to drive themselves to the hotel because they plan to stay the night with their dates. There is no need to worry about them drinking and driving because they will spend the night in the hotel. However, you know that your national officers do not permit overnight events.

- What are the issues in this case?
- What are your options for handling the situation? How might each option play out? Which option do you prefer?
- Is it really a big deal to let a few seniors spend the night? What would happen if something bad happened to them at the hotel? What would happen if a sister was assaulted? Who would be responsible?
- What should you do if other members of the chapter decide that they also want to spend the night? Where do you draw the line?
- How hard is it as a junior to say no to seniors?
- Why don't your national offices allow overnight events?

## Reindeer Games

As a joke, each December four sorority women take two reindeer from the lawn of one particular community member and pose them in sexual positions. They have been doing this for three years. Their senior year they return to the house to carry on their tradition, and the homeowner is waiting on the front porch to catch them in the act. First, he calls the police. Then he calls the president of the university, who in turn calls the dean of students. Two of the sorority women are also RAs. They are immediately fired from their positions even though they were great staff members. As president of your chapter, you need to decide how to deal with the four members.

- What are the issues in this case?
- What are your options for handling the situation? How might each option play out? Which option do you prefer?
- Would it make a difference if the four members had never been in trouble before? Would it make a difference if this was their only deviant act? Would it make a difference if you know that they are not stellar members of your chapter and are not surprised that they pulled this prank?

## One Cold Winter Evening

Four of the sophomores in your chapter decide to have a little fun with four of the new members. At 1:00 A.M. on a Wednesday, they call the new members and demand that they meet them outside their residence hall in fifteen minutes. The new members comply and are immediately ushered into an SUV. They are blindfolded and driven around for about thirty minutes. After this time the blindfolds are removed and the new members are forced out of the car. The women are in the middle of a field at 1:30 A.M. on a cold January night. They are handed a fifth of vodka and instructed to drink it and find their way back to campus. The active members inform them that this is a bonding experience. They jump back into the SUV and take off, leaving the new members stranded in below-freezing temperatures. The new members are terrified and quickly become very cold. One does not have gloves, and none of them are wearing warm boots. Because of a series of wrong turns, it takes them four hours to find their way back to campus— which is only two miles away. They arrive freezing, crying, and ready to quit the chapter. One thinks she has frostbite. They call your room immediately and inform you of the incident.

- What are the issues in this case?
- What are your options for handling the situation? How might each option play out? Which option do you prefer?
- How do you think the active members would have felt if the same thing had been done to them when they were new members?
- Would it make a difference if the active members had been nearby observing the new members and claimed that they would have intervened if the new members had gotten into serious trouble?
- Do you inform your Greek advisor/national office of the incident? What would happen if this incident got reported to the college and it reported it to your national officers? Could this incident shut down your chapter? Can the behavior of four members fall on the shoulders of an entire chapter?
- What will happen if one or more of the new members have been seriously hurt as a result of the hazing incident, for example losing toes to frostbite, or experiencing alcohol poisoning?
- What are the implications if the new members' parents get involved and threaten to sue you and the chapter?

# Brrr . . .

Your fraternity has heating issues. You have an older house and the members don't take good care of it. The top floor doesn't have windows and your heat has been shut off because someone didn't pay the heating bill. Despite the potential fire hazard, members are using space heaters to keep warm. The Greek advisor finds out about your current heating problems and demands that the chapter get the house up to code immediately. You ignore his request and he has no choice but to call the fire marshal, who condemns the house.

- What are the issues in this case?
- What are your options for handling the situation? How might each option play out? Which option do you prefer?
- How could you have prevented the condemnation of your house? What role does your housing corporation play in the upkeep of your house?
- How might you be able to reallocate funds to make the necessary repairs?
- What are the pros and cons associated with having a chapter house?

## Who Invited *That* Guy?

Your chapter holds a big party Saturday night in your chapter house. Those at the door ignore the guest list and let anyone in. Some guy enters the party and has a couple of beers. He starts making racially inappropriate comments that are overheard by some of the brothers. They are immediately offended and remove him from the party. One chapter member takes things a step further and starts beating him up in the middle of the street.

- What are the issues in this case?
- What are your options for handling the situation? How might each option play out? Which option do you prefer?
- What is the purpose of a guest list? Should you admit people whom you don't know to your parties?
- What are the risks involved in serving the uninvited person alcohol?
- If the uninvited person decides to press charges against the members who beat him, who will be responsible?

## Come Out Already

You are 99 percent sure that one of your chapter members is gay. The entire chapter also believes he is gay, but he hasn't come out to the chapter. The chapter is okay with him being gay, and you want to tell him that. You want him to feel comfortable coming out and want him to be himself within the chapter.

- What are the issues in this case?
- What are your options for handling the situation? How might each option play out? Which option do you prefer?
- What would be the consequences of you telling him that it is okay to come out and him telling you that he isn't gay?
- Is it ever okay to force someone to reveal his or her sexuality?

## Letters to a Strip Club

One of the most important rules that goes with being a brother in Delta Phi Omicron fraternity is to wear your letters in a respectful manner. As stated explicitly in the fraternity charter, "Brothers will not engage in self-destructive or disrespectful behavior while representing the fraternity with letters on their person." The statement seems to be interpreted differently during each executive team's tenure, and currently the group has not had any discussions about how to interpret it.

James and Tyler, both active members, are invited to attend a former brother's bachelor party off campus during the summer before their senior year. The men golf, have dinner, visit a few bars, and decide to go to a local gentleman's club before turning in. Both James and Tyler become quite intoxicated as the night goes on. Bob, also an active member, comes up to James at the end of the evening and notices that the T-shirt under his polo has fraternity letters on it. He asks James if he is aware that he is wearing the shirt, and James replies that he just grabbed the shirt without really looking at it.

In August, when James returns to move into the Delta Phi Omicron house, he notices a blue sheet on his bunk. Getting a blue sheet means that a brother has turned you in to the executive board for a charter violation. James is confused, because he does not believe he has done anything wrong. He will not be able to find out what the violation is until the charter's first meeting is held the next week. At the meeting, James is given the following charge: "Wearing Delta Phi Omicron fraternity letters while engaging in disrespectful behavior to women." James responds, "You have got to be kidding me. I did not even know I had the shirt on, and the letters were not even showing."

- What are the issues in this case?
- What are the options for handling the situation? How might each option play out? Which option do you prefer?
- Do you think Bob had another motive for turning James in? Does he have some responsibility here?

## Higher-ups in Sorority Smoking Marijuana

Each year the Sigma Delta sorority leaves campus for an overnight retreat. All members in good standing with the sorority are invited, and the executive board and recent alumni plan team-building activities. The goals of the retreat are to bring together the women who are members and promote team building. The retreat is held at a Girl Scouts of America cabin.

The women arrive on Friday afternoon and get settled into the cabin, which is nestled in a remote area with nice walking trails and a lake that has canoes and kayaks available. Later, Barb, Sarah, and Toni, all new sisters in the sorority, decide to walk down to the lake and pass some time before the structured activities begin. On their way there, Toni asks, "Do you hear that giggling?" Sarah replies, "I hear something, but where is it coming from?" Toni says, "Let's find out." As they walk a bit closer to the woods, they see Pam, the current president of the sorority; Jodi, the vice president; and Aimee, a recent graduate and past president just inside the edge of the woods smoking marijuana. Sarah whispers, "We'd better get out of here before they see us." The three get out of earshot and stop to discuss what they just saw. Barb, Sarah, and Toni have just finished the pledging process, which emphasizes behavior and representation of self and sorority. Barb says, "What do we do? My big sister and I discussed this kind of behavior, and she said that in the past women have had their letters taken away for participating in illegal activities while at a sorority function." Sarah asks, "Should we tell someone?" Toni replies, "Well, whom are we going to tell if the three most powerful women in the sorority are all involved?"

- What are the issues in this case?
- What are Toni, Sarah, and Barb's options for handling the situation? How might each option play out? Which option do you prefer?

## CASES APPROPRIATE FOR INTERFRATERNITY COUNCIL LEADERS AND PANHELLENIC PRESIDENTS

## Promising Bids

During formal recruitment, three women suddenly drop out. As the Panhellenic recruitment chair, you are surprised because you know that they were eager to join a sorority. When you ask one of them why she dropped out, she claims that she is just too busy and will consider informal recruitment next semester. After formal recruitment commenced, all three women were offered a bid to a chapter through continuous open bidding (COB). All of the women accepted and joined the chapter. You are suspicious that the chapter encouraged the women to drop out of formal recruitment and promised them a bid during COB. This way they could make quota and then use the COB process to reach chapter total. This behavior is a form of promising a bid and is a recruitment infraction.

- What are the issues in this case?
- What are your options for handling the situation? How might each option play out? Which option do you prefer?
- What should you do if you don't have any evidence that the chapter promised bids and the three women deny any such arrangement?
- What should you do if one of the women admits that they were advised to drop out of formal recruitment? How do you discipline the chapter? The three new members?
- How do you prevent this from happening in the future?

## One Bad Apple

One fraternity will not play by the rules and is bringing down the Greek reputation. Members do not attend Interfraternity Council (IFC) meetings, they are on social probation for having a keg party, they are known to do drugs, they often come to class drunk while wearing their letters, they don't do any philanthropic events, they play pranks on other chapters, and they disappoint their Greek-week partners with their lack of participation. Although they are not productive members of the Greek system, they do have the highest GPA. Whenever they get into trouble, they always point out that fact. You are the new IFC president and you are fed up with their behavior. You want them to either clean up their act or get kicked off campus.

- What are the issues in this case?
- What are your options for handling the situation? How might each option play out? Which option do you prefer?
- What should you do if you confront the chapter president and he won't do anything about the behavior?
- What should you do if you contact the national office and it won't do anything?
- Should you get administration involved? If so, what should you do if administration knows that the chapter isn't great but is not willing to undergo the hassle of removing the chapter members from campus?

## Contributing to the Greek Image

One of the fraternities on campus is known for its public hazing displays. Active members are often seen yelling orders at new members. The new-member class is instructed to do calisthenics in the middle of the quad, forced to dress like women one day, and carry matches at all times in the event that an active member wants them to recite the fraternity creed or Greek alphabet before the match extinguishes. The entire campus is aware of the fraternity's antics but no one does anything about it. Recently, the campus newspaper runs an article about Greek hazing and cites the chapter's many offenses. It criticizes the Greek system and questions the value of fraternities' contributions to the campus community. It also chastises the administration for looking the other way.

- What are the issues in this case?
- What are your options for handling the situation? How might each option play out? Which option do you prefer?
- Is any hazing okay? Why do you think this hazing is permitted? Where do you draw the line? What would happen if a fraternity member collapsed during the calisthenics and had to be rushed to the hospital?
- What is the role of the Panhellenic Council and IFC in disciplining chapters for hazing?
- How are fraternities and sororities on your campus perceived? What do you think contributes to this perception? Is the perception accurate? What suggestions do you have for promoting a more positive Greek image on your campus?

# Dry Recruitment?

For the first time, all the fraternities agree that formal recruitment parties will not include alcohol. One chapter disagreed with this new policy but was outvoted by the others. It disagreed because it is the chapter known for throwing the best parties and the chapter members didn't know how to host an alcohol-free event. Rather than comply with the new policy, the chapter holds its recruitment event off campus and the members serve alcohol. Potential members attend and then tell the other chapters about the great event. One of the chapters reports the event to the IFC.

- What are the issues in this case?
- What are the options for handling the situation? How might each option play out? Which option do you prefer?
- Why is it unwise to serve alcohol at recruitment events? How many of the potential new members would be age twenty-one? What message does serving alcohol at a recruitment event send?
- How can the IFC hold the chapter accountable? How could the IFC have prevented the violation of policy? Does your IFC send monitors

to recruitment events? What alternatives to serving alcohol are there for recruitment events?

## Gung Ho for Greek Week

One sorority on your campus is obsessed with Greek week. It rarely wins any academic, leadership, or philanthropic awards as a sorority, but it *always* wins Greek week. It encourages chapter members to skip class if necessary to practice for or attend Greek-week events. The chapter members practice their Greek song until 3:00 A.M. every night of Greek week. They often skip class or even come to class intoxicated because they were up so late the night before. They also have the added pressure by alumni to win. They go wild if they win an event and often shed tears if they don't win. The rest of the chapters are so sick of their competitive attitude that they will do anything just to see them lose. Midway through Greek week, one of the chapters puts a large sign on its roof claiming that the competitive sorority is a "bunch of Nazis." Although most of the Greeks think it is funny, the Jewish members are extremely offended. They see this as just another example of anti-Semitism.

- What are the issues in this case?
- What are the options for handling the situation? How might each option play out? Which option do you prefer?
- Who should handle this situation, the Greek-week committee, the Panhellenic Council, or the IFC?
- Who should address the competitive chapter? Why do you think it is so competitive? Should alumni be involved in the solution? How would you handle irate alumni?
- Is the chapter that displayed the sign subject to any disciplinary action?
- Should you address the Jewish Greeks? How would you use this incident to help educate the larger community about the inappropriateness of these members' actions? If you decide to hold a forum to discuss Judaism, should you require all members to attend? Does forced participation address the issue?

# Greek Cleanup

Each Greek week the fraternities and sororities participate in a community service project where they pick up the trash off the streets of the surrounding community. Every year Greeks complain about the event. They don't enjoy doing the cleanup and don't think the community members appreciate it. They only participate because their chapter will fine them if they don't. This year's Greek-week chairperson brings up the event to the planning committee. Although the committee agrees that the event isn't well received, no one can think of an alternative. The committee puts it on the schedule again for this year.

- What are the issues in this case?
- What are your options for handling the situation? How might each option play out? Which option do you prefer?
- What is the purpose of community service or your other philanthropic events? Why do some members get more out of the experience than others?
- Why do you think the committee couldn't come up with an alternative event? Do you think a different type of event might be more meaningful for the participants?
- What is the purpose of fining your members? Are there any alternatives to fining that will motivate your members to attend events? Do you think fining motivates them?

# "Bonging" on Facebook

Your Greek advisor brings to your attention the Facebook accounts of a number of underage fraternity and sorority members. On their Facebooks is a series of pictures. In them the Greek members are wearing their letters while "bonging" beers, doing shots, and in one case smoking marijuana. Many of the pictures are taken at chapter-sponsored events, which is obvious because the the events are identified in the captions. These pictures are evidence of underage drinking at chapter events, a violation of university policy. The Greek advisor wants the chapters taken through the conduct process.

- What are the issues in this case?
- What are your options for handling the situation? How might each option play out? Which option do you prefer?
- What would you do if your chapter was one of the chapters involved?
- When are you an individual and when are you a member of your Greek organization? Should your entire chapter be punished for what individual members post on their Facebook account? How do you tell the chapters that they need to clean up their online image?

## Hazing in the Digital Age

Vanessa is a new member in your chapter and she lives with Gabriella, a new member from another chapter. Gabriella tells Vanessa that last weekend three new members were invited to pre-party with some active members. The active members informed them that they had a new-member challenge for them. The new members were each given three shots of liquor and then handed a digital camera. They were informed that they had two hours to take pictures of ten penises. If they didn't accomplish the task they would have to clean the active members' apartment until they were initiated. The new members were very uncomfortable with the request but did as they were told. After hearing this account of the hazing, Vanessa decides to call her new-member educator to report the incident. Gabriella knows that she's been hazed and she doesn't want it to happen to anyone else, but because she doesn't want to get her chapter in trouble, she won't officially report the incident.

- What are the issues in this case?
- What are your options for handling the situation? How might each option play out? Which option do you prefer?
- What would you do if the active members are members of your chapter? Would you be more or less harsh? Would you choose to handle the incident internally? If the active members are your friends, what would you do?
- What would you do if the active members are from another chapter?

## Is It Okay to Fail?

You are struggling to get members of the Panhellenic Council to help with programming. For most of the semester, you shoulder much of the responsibility. You try to delegate but follow-through is not strong, and it seems you always have to step in and save the event. You have had enough! The group decides to sponsor a Greek movie night. You delegate the planning and implementation to four members of the council. You sit back and watch the planning. The promotional materials are uninspiring. The movie that they select isn't interesting. You can tell that the event is going to be a disaster. You resist the urge to intervene. Only five people attend the event, and the organization wastes $200.

- What are the issues in this case?
- What are your options for handling the situation? How might each option play out? Which option do you prefer?
- Should you have intervened? What message would that have sent?
- Are there times when you feel like you are the only one in your organization who does anything? Can this pressure lead to anxiety? Burnout? Frustration?
- Is it possible to learn from the experience and have it be a turning point for the organization? Would it change things if the members apologize for the way they handled the event and sincerely offer a higher level of investment in the future?
- Is it sometimes okay to fail?

## Tailgating, Anyone?

The IFC and Panhellenic Council work together to plan a one-day Greek leadership conference on campus. A national officer from each chapter is in attendance, and the national officers are facilitating most of the sessions. The leadership conference is held the same day as a home football game, and many of the chapters elect to get drunk at the tailgate rather than attend the conference. Consequently, many send only their new members. The national officers are very discouraged by the lack of participation.

- What are the issues in this case?
- What are your options for handling the situation? How might each option play out? Which option do you prefer?
- How would you address the poor attendance this year?
- What would you do next year to ensure better attendance other than plan around home football games?

# We Love Kegs

The IFC agrees that all fraternities are invited to give a ten-minute presentation highlighting the strengths of their chapter during Greek information night. One fraternity decides to present a slide show. The members show a picture of the back of a truck full of kegs and other pictures of members consuming alcohol. They clearly are sending a message that they like to party. As the IFC recruitment chair, you are very upset with their slide show. The vice president of student affairs is in attendance at the recruitment event. He is known to be anti-Greek and expresses his concern about the message that this chapter is sending to potential new members.

- What are the issues in this case?
- What are the options for handling the situation? How might each option play out? Which option do you prefer?
- How should you address the incident with the chapter? How could you improve next year's information night?
- Are there some chapters on your campus who are not positive contributors to the Greek system? Does their party reputation negatively taint the rest of the Greek system? What can you do to alter their behavior?

# No One Wants to Talk

Your school lacks Greek unity. There is a great deal of competition among Greek chapters on your campus. As a result, no one wants to speak during

Panhellenic or IFC meetings. The representatives have been given strict orders not to air their chapter's dirty laundry at the meetings. They also are not eager to collaborate on any projects. As the president, you are completely frustrated. How can you get anything accomplished this year if no one will talk?

- What are the issues in this case?
- What are your options for handling the situation? How might each option play out? Which option do you prefer?
- Is Greek unity important? Why or why not? What would happen if there was no support for one another and for the systems as a whole?

## Greek-Week Chair, Anyone?

Each year, one male and one female chapter member are appointed Greek-week co-chairs. This year only one male and one female applied for the positions. Applications were taken for three weeks. Announcements were made at chapter meetings as well as at IFC and Panhellenic meetings, they were posted on the Greek Website, and a letter was sent to all chapter presidents. Multiple reminders were also issued. The Panhellenic Council is frustrated with the turnout. The IFC does not want to extend the deadline. However, last year the deadline was extended, so the Panhellenic Council wants to do the same this year. The strongest advocate for the extension is a female member of the council who wants to apply for the position. The strongest advocate for keeping the deadline is the male who applied to be a co-chair and who is also a member of the IFC.

- What are the issues in this case?
- What are your options for handling the situation? How might each option play out? Which option do you prefer?
- Could you have done anything else to solicit more applicants? If you choose to extend the deadline for a second year in a row, what message will you be sending?
- What should you do if you are not happy with the two applicants? What should you do if you are satisfied with the two applicants?

## Fines, Fines, and More Fines

As the vice president of the IFC you need the names and contact information for the officers of the chapters. You ask the IFC delegates to bring the information to the next IFC meeting. Only half of the delegates bring the information. You warn the other chapters that if they don't get you the information by the next week you will fine the chapter fifty dollars. The following week three chapters still do not have the information, so you fine them.

- What are the issues in this case?
- What are the options for handling the situation? How might each option play out? Which option do you prefer?
- Are there any other ways that you can get the information without fining the chapters? What purpose does fining the chapters serve?

## We've Always Done It This Way

You are the Panhellenic president on a predominantly commuter campus. You have four sororities. The total members allowed per sorority is sixty and all chapters are well below that number, with the largest chapter having thirty-five members and the smallest having eighteen. Your current recruitment practices do not work. You require commuters to come back to campus for four days over the course of a long weekend, and if they fail to attend all four days, they cannot participate. This structure is very limiting given your population of students. Consequently, participation dwindles every year.

You and the Greek advisor decide to advocate for a partially structured recruitment. Your new idea is a prolonged recruitment period during which potential new members can participate at any time until preference night. The new structure involves a series of open houses over two weeks. Each of the four chapters on your campus sponsors five recruitment events or open houses that last one hour each. Chapters may use the middle thirty minutes for a presentation, a skit, or another activity. Potential members are required to attend at least two recruitment events for each chapter. After that time, potential new members are invited to preference teas; they may attend two of these. After the teas, potential new members sign preference cards and the normal bid-matching process occurs.

You are really excited about this new strategy and are confident that it will work well on your campus. It is a more sincere approach to recruitment and allows potential new members and chapters to spend more time getting to know each other. Now you need to get the Panhellenic Council and the recruitment chairs on board. However, they are resistant to the change, because no one has ever tried to recruit new members this way.

- What are the issues in this case?
- What are your options for handling the situation? How might each option play out? Which option do you prefer?
- How hesitant would you be to make changes to your current recruitment strategies? How confident are you that the new strategy will work on your campus? What would your reaction be if your campus implemented the strategy and it was so successful that it doubled the size of its chapters?

## Defend Yourself

The president of your college/university requests that the fraternities and sororities provide a written statement detailing how they support the mission and vision of the university. The groups are angered by this request and feel that they are being targeted. The president didn't request similar documentation from any of the other student organizations. None of the other organizations are being held accountable like the Greeks. You believe that if your organization's integrity is in question, then the president should also question the integrity of other groups as well. You know that these other groups are far from perfect.

- What are the issues in this case?
- What are your options for handling the situation? How might each option play out? Which option do you prefer?
- Are Greeks on your campus under a microscope? Why do you think the Greeks in this case are subject to additional scrutiny? Do you think the scrutiny is warranted?

## Involvement of All Greeks

You want to involve members of the historically Black fraternities and sororities in Greek week. Because their groups are much smaller than the predominantly White fraternities and sororities, you need to find a fair way to include them. You decide to pair chapters so that each team consists of eighty members. For them to participate, they ask that you reevaluate some of your Greek games. Rather than have a lip-sync event, they prefer a variety show. They also ask that you eliminate the water games. Your planning committee is divided on the requests.

- What are the issues in this case?
- What are your options for handling the situation? How might each option play out? Which option do you prefer?
- Why is it important to include the National Panhellenic Council groups in Greek week? Why are they asking you to change some of the events?
- How much do you know about the historically Black chapters on your campus? Why do the groups know so little about each other?
- Do the predominantly White chapters on your campus have members who are persons of color? Why or why not? Would you consider your chapters inclusive? Diverse?

## The Keg Stand

At an all-Greek recruitment event, one of the chapters is serving root beer from a keg. The event is slow, and the chapter members are bored. One of them suggests doing keg stands on the root beer keg. They ask permission from the IFC chair and because no one else is around he agrees. You are the Panhellenic chair and you, along with ten potential new members who enter the event with you, witness the keg stands. The Greek advisor also sees the stands and is upset with the chapter.

- What are the issues in this case?
- What are your options for handling the situation? How might each option play out? Which option do you prefer?

- What message does doing keg stands at a recruitment event send to potential new members?

## Step Down or Else

Two months into your term as the Panhellenic president, your advisor brings a letter to the Panhellenic meeting. He hands you the letter and asks you to read it. The anonymous letter claims that you are a horrible leader. The authors state that you are ineffective at goal setting, that you have turned the Panhellenic Council into the Greek police, and that your ego is too large for the position. The letter goes on to say that you have to read the letter to the larger group or else the authors will. You walk into the Panhellenic meeting obviously upset. Approximately half your chapter is in attendance. You ask the authors of the letter to identify themselves. Both are members of the executive board, and one is a member of your sorority. The two demand your resignation. The members of your chapter appear to be present to support your resignation.

- What are the issues in this case?
- What are your options for handling the situation? How might each option play out? Which option do you prefer?
- If you choose to resign, how should you handle your chapter after this meeting?
- Since this is the first you have heard of the members' discontent and you really want to try to redeem yourself, what could you do to change the members' minds?
- If you were not the president but another executive board member, what would you do?
- What do you need from your advisor?

# 6

# LEADING MINORITY/ UNDERREPRESENTED GROUPS CASES

## Don't Do Anything

L emont, an African American student living on your residence hall floor, is not liked by his three White roommates. Throughout the semester the animosity toward Lemont escalates. Late one Thursday night, someone paints on Lemont's door, "I can't stand coons." Lemont is confident that his roommates are responsible for the act. He tells you, the resident assistant (RA), "I don't want to do anything about this because it will only make things worse for me. It's really no big deal. I'll just wash it off and we'll forget about it." You know as an RA you must file an incident report.

- What are the issues in this case?
- What are your options for handling the situation? How might each option play out? Which option do you prefer?
- How should you address it with the roommates?
- Since most of your residents know about the incident, how should you address it with your floor?

## Derogatory Remarks during a Campus Tour

You are giving a campus tour to your orientation group. Two male students pass your group holding hands. One of the students in your group yells out, "Fags!"

- What are the issues in this case?
- What are your options for handling the situation? How might each option play out? Which option do you prefer?
- If earlier in the day another member of the orientation group informed you that he is gay, are you now obligated to say something?
- Would the student's inappropriate comment prompt you to discuss other inappropriate words or phrases (e.g., "queer," "spic," the "n" word, "Jew them down," "Indian giver")?

## Racial Comments during a Class Project

Philosophy classes at Major Community College have student leaders who facilitate and direct a portion of the class. At the beginning of the year, a group of faculty select the leaders from the top students from the previous year. Steve and Alanya are selected to lead Dr. Warden's class during the fall semester. The two are doing an excellent job assisting with group projects and have even helped record graded papers for Dr. Warden. During a Tuesday session of class, Steve and Alanya are helping the groups plan their class projects, and Dr. Warden decides to walk around and monitor. As he approaches the group that Steve is working with, he hears Steve say, "Well, just Jew him down in price—that is way too much." There is an audible gasp from the other students in the group after he makes this comment.

- What are the issues in this case?
- What are Dr. Warden's options for handling the situation? How might each option play out? Which option do you prefer?

## Nathan or Natalie?

You are one of two lead orientation leaders at your school. You assumed this responsibility because of your great success as an orientation leader the previous year. One of your responsibilities is to review the orientation registration forms and place the new students into orientation groups. One of the registration forms states that once the student's parents drop him off at orientation, the student is to go by the name Natalie rather than Nathan. This is your first exposure to a transgender person and you are not sure what to do. You approach your advisor and he talks you through your options. The two of you agree that you want Natalie's orientation experience to be positive and want her to feel comfortable on campus, but you are worried about some of the reactions of other new students.

- What are the issues in this case?
- What are your options for handling the situation? How might each option play out? Which option do you prefer?
- If Natalie is indeed transgender and wants to start her new life on campus as a woman, what resources are available on your campus to support her?
- What advice or recommendations might you have for her?
- Should you consider educating the staff on issues related to sexual orientation and transgender? Do you have a particular orientation leader in mind to facilitate Natalie's group? Should you inform the leader of Natalie's request?

## Who Sprayed the Pepper Spray?

The Latino Student Organization is a large group that is quite active on campus and inclusive of many different ethnicities. Although the group is inclusive, there are some tensions between some of the groups of students that frequent the organization's events. At the spring formal that the organization is hosting at a local banquet hall, tensions between two of the groups come to a head, and someone at the party sprays pepper spray into the crowd of 112 students. The banquet center is evacuated, and two students are injured by the rush and taken to a local hospital. You are the current president of the Latino Student Organization, and you have been asked by the Office of Student Affairs and the university president to report who sprayed the pepper spray. If you don't do this the group will lose all privileges as a student group on campus.

- What are the issues in this case?
- What are your options for handling the situation? How might each option play out? Which option do you prefer?
- What should you do if the individual(s) responsible do not come forward? What should you do if the individual(s) responsible are not affiliated with the group or the university?

## Should I Come Out or Stay in the Closet?

Burtch University, a private liberal arts school in scenic Colorado, is home to one of the best residential life programs in the country. Each year the university and the Office of Residence Life win numerous awards for their programs and management of facilities. The Office of Residence Life is also known for graduating some of the best student affairs graduate students in the country. These graduates are sought out by other schools around the country.

Bob is a freshman at Burtch and going through the process of applying for a position with residence life. He is interested in going on to a graduate program in student affairs after he earns his bachelor's degree and feels that having residence life experience will give him a great foundation. While filling out the application, he reads that the Office of Residence Life does not hire individuals who are openly gay, lesbian, or bisexual. Bob is quite surprised that Burtch has such a policy, and as a gay man, he is offended. Bob has only recently come out to his family. He is still working through his own identity issues and is not ready to come out to his college peers yet.

Bob is not sure what to do. He knows that he will come out to his college peers someday and even hopes to have a partner with whom he can share the college experience. He knows the university has a strong gay and lesbian alliance and has a renowned queer studies program. He really wants to get a job with residence life, because he knows that being affiliated with such a strong program will help him get into a great graduate program in the future. He also wants to be true to who he is and cannot imagine living a closeted life throughout his college tenure.

- What are the issues in this case?
- What are Bob's options for handling the situation? How might each option play out? Which option do you prefer?

- What are the potential issues that Bob will face if he proceeds with the application process?
- How should Bob proceed with the application process? If Bob decides to reveal his sexuality and challenge the policy, how should he proceed?

# Disrespectful Leadership

Seth and Kim are the co-presidents of the National Society of Black Philosophers (NSBP). The NSBP is an academic group for minority philosophy students. Seth is a third-year African American student who was born in New York City. He is an excellent student who plans to go to graduate school at an Ivy League school. He takes great pride in his academic success and also works hard in his leadership and co-curricular activities. Kim is a fourth-year student from the Dominican Republic. She is a light-skinned Black woman who has been in the United States since she was four years old. She has her green card and plans to stay after graduating. Kim is also a good student and wants to attend a highly ranked graduate school. Being co-president is her first elected leadership role and she is excited about working with Seth. She has heard very good things about his leadership style from others in the group.

The first major task for Seth and Kim as co-presidents is to set the meeting and activities schedule for the year. Both students do not subscribe to the position that they do things a certain way because they have always been done that way. Seth is a bit more outgoing than Kim, so they decide in the beginning that he will take the lead at the meetings and she will be in more of a supportive role. The first meeting goes well until Seth begins talking about their events for the year. Kim is a bit confused because they had decided together that they would discuss the events with the other executive team members before making any decisions. When Seth finishes talking Kim says, "These are just ideas, and we are certainly open to your thoughts and suggestions." Seth replies, "We can change a bit but most are pretty set in stone." Kim is quite humiliated by the remark but decides to wait until after the meeting when they are alone to voice her concerns.

As Seth starts packing up to go after the meeting, Kim approaches him even though the secretary and member at large are still in the room. She says,

"I am confused by your statement about the upcoming events. I was under the impression that we were going to discuss these events more and decide as a group how we wanted to use our resources." Seth replies, "You know, I do not appreciate a half-Black person questioning my authority in front of my peers. You have overstepped your bounds and I am not going to put up with it anymore. I think you should step down as co-president."

- What are the issues in this case?
- What are Kim's options for handling the situation? How might each option play out? Which option do you prefer?
- Should Kim step down? If not, what could she do to improve their working relationship?
- What office(s) should Kim go to for advice in this situation?
- How did Seth violate his role as co-president as well as his role as a leader and mentor of the younger members?

## College Looks Other Way Regarding Racially Biased Honor Society

Susie is a Latino student majoring in English at Pressview Community College (PCC) and is thinking about joining an honor society for students with a grade point average (GPA) of 3.5 or higher. She is currently a sophomore with a 3.93 GPA. Joe is the president of Delta Omicron, an honor society at PCC. He is also cochair for recruitment and initiation.

On Tuesday, Delta Omicron has a recruitment event in the student union. Susie has heard about the event and decides to visit the society's table and get some information. Joe is working the table when she and four other students approach him. Susie happens to be the only minority female in the group. Joe begins talking with two of the male students. He takes extra care to give them Delta Omicron literature and invitations to upcoming rush events, and he also takes their contact information. Before the two men walk away, Susie notices that Joe has given them each a green flyer that Susie does not see on the table. The next two students, who are Caucasian males, get the same extensive treatment and also the "secret" green flyer. As Susie finds herself alone at the table with Joe, she gets excited that it is her turn to meet with him. He asks her a little bit about herself, but as she begins to talk he cuts her off and gives her the literature from the table. Joe then begins talking to a woman he clearly knows well. Frustrated and not sure what to think, Susie walks away.

Later that day, Susie is at her desk job in the student life office. Her supervisor, Dr. Donna Jackson, associate dean of student life, asks her why she seems a bit down. She explains what she experienced at the Delta Omicron table and how this has upset her because the group would be such a great one for her to join. Susie says she is not sure if Joe was ignoring her intentionally or if he just got busy.

Dr. Jackson asks Susie to come into her office so she can shed some light on the situation. The dean shares with Susie that Delta Omicron has historically been an organization that only initiates students who are White. Susie is flabbergasted and asks how the administration at PCC can let this go on. The dean explains that because the group does so much service for the college, the administration tends to look the other way. Susie begins to question this, but Dean Jackson tells her that it is a battle not worth fighting. Susie leaves the meeting quite upset and not sure what to do.

- What are the issues in this case?
- What are Susie's options for handling the situation? How might each option play out? Which option do you prefer?
- What office(s) should Susie start with? Who may be her allies?
- Should Susie try going directly to Delta Omicron leadership? If so, whom should she talk to in the group?
- In what ways is PCC being unethical? In what ways is Delta Omicron being unethical?

# Hate E-mail

Lena is the resident hall director (RHD) of Canary Hall at League University. She is a second-year graduate student and has a staff of six hall directors who directly report to her. Chen is the hall director on 2A, which is the male wing of the hall. All year 2A has been a troublesome floor. Lena and Chen have had to make numerous judicial referrals for damage, noise, alcohol, and disruptive behavior. Lena has even challenged Chen to think of different ways to constructively engage his residents.

Chen and Lena have always had a good working relationship, but outside work they have little to nothing in common. During the first few weeks of school, Lena and Chen had a discussion about appropriate behavior in social settings outside the hall. Chen said that it should not matter what he does when not on duty, but Lena said that he is still a role model and needs to act like one. Since then their relationship has been chilly, but they have been cordial during hall meetings and programs.

During the final three weeks of the semester, behavior on floor 2A and in Canary Hall goes from bad to worse. Chen is often absent from the hall and his floor, and his colleagues are left picking up the slack. He serves his assigned duty times but does little else to support his peers.

One day while checking her e-mail, Lena gets a message that has no subject line and appears to have come from an address that mass-produces e-mails. She opens the e-mail and cannot believe what she sees. The message is riddled with hateful statements about her being an incompetent lesbian who cannot run a building. All she can think of is why someone would be sending this to her. Lena is not sure whom she should call first, but she finally decides to call Julia, her good friend and a fellow RHD. Julia has never seen Lena so rattled and tells her to call the public safety department. Lena does so and files a complaint. The person whom Lena speaks with in public safety says that sending hate mail is a federal offense and that someone could be in a lot of trouble.

Later, Lena has difficulty studying for her finals. She is distracted because of the disturbing e-mail. She has her suspicions about the authors but must let due process run its course. She knows that Chen is a computer science major and very good with computers. Ten of the male residents on his floor are also good with computers but are not computer science majors. Any one of them could have sent the e-mail.

After dinner, Julia comes into Lena's office and tells her that she heard some students talking in the cafeteria about an e-mail that they had sent to their boss. Chen and Tom, another hall director in their building, were sitting among this group of students.

- What are the issues in this case?
- What are Lena's options for handling the situation? How might each option play out? Which option do you prefer?
- If Lena confronts Chen and Tom but it is found that they are not the authors of the e-mail, what should she do?

## Big Fish, Small Pond

Lamar is a brand-new freshman at Gorge City State College (GCSC). It is a small school in the Colorado River Valley. GCSC is home to one of the most active Native American student groups in the Rocky Mountain region. The group is so active that the admissions office often uses its members and activities in recruiting potential students. Lamar selected GCSC because he wishes to become a member of the group and he was very excited when he was admitted to the college.

Lamar was very active in high school. He was president of his senior class, captain of both the football and golf teams, and an active member of the National Honor Society. His high school did not have any organization for Native American students, but he is proud of his heritage and wants to be involved with an associated group.

Lamar attends the first group meeting of the Native American student group and is excited to see more than fifty students there. At the end of the meeting, he goes to the front of the room to talk with the president. The president is nice and tells Lamar to write his name and contact information on a sheet of paper so that the board can get in touch with him when it is looking to fill positions. Lamar does so and then begins telling the president about all the activities that he was involved in while in high school. The president is interested but after fifteen minutes says he has to go. Lamar feels a bit slighted but chalks it up to the president being busy.

After a week, Lamar does not hear from the board so he goes to the organization's Website to find some contact information. He calls the faculty advisor and leaves a message. When another week goes by and he still does not hear from anyone, he gets anxious and goes to visit the faculty advisor. Lamar firmly believes that since he was such a superstar student leader in high school, the group will certainly want him for a leadership role. When Lamar finds that the advisor is not in his office, Lamar gets upset and leaves a curt note asking the advisor to call and saying that he feels the advisor is being rude. After the advisor reads the note, he decides to take it to the next group meeting. At the meeting he reads it aloud and then advises that all members who come into contact with Lamar be careful, because he is a loose cannon.

- What are the issues in this case?
- What are the group's options for handling the situation? How might each option play out? Which option do you prefer?
- Do you think the group has any obligation to work with Lamar on improving his attitude? Should the group advise him on how he can be an effective college leader?
- What could Lamar do to improve his relationship with the group as well as his chances of being selected for a leadership position?

## Poor Turnout for the Martin Luther King, Jr. Celebration

Each year the Office of Institutional Diversity and a student committee coordinate the Martin Luther King, Jr. celebration. The celebration typically lasts ninety minutes and features a prominent speaker, a student speech, and ethnic dancers followed by a reception. Classes are canceled during the celebration so that students, faculty, and staff can attend.

This year, despite great publicity and a well-known speaker, attendance is very low. The venue seats 1,000 and only about 150 attend the event. Of particular concern, very few African American students attend. As the president of the African American Student Alliance, you are particularly disturbed by the lack of participation. You find yourself wondering, "Where were all the African American students? Why didn't they care enough to attend this significant event? How will their lack of participation reflect on how others perceive African American students on our campus?"

- What are the issues in this case?
- What are your options for handling the situation? How might each option play out? Which option do you prefer?
- Why do you think the community didn't attend the event? What are your suggestions for improving attendance next year?
- Have you ever struggled to get people to attend your events? How have you motivated people in the past?

# Kiss-Off

James, a very proud and outwardly gay male, is a junior at Ludington University. He is the coordinator of National Coming Out Week for his Gay, Lesbian, Bi, Transgender, Queer (GLBTQ) Organization. Ludington is a large, private Catholic university, and given its religious affiliation, it does not "officially" recognize the GLBTQ. This angers many members of the organization, especially James.

James and the other members of the organization get together to discuss what they should do to get the university to recognize their group. He argues, "Administration can't continue to ignore our organization. They are living in the dark ages. We need to do something very visible for Coming Out Week. Something they can't ignore. I think we should have a kiss-off. Gay and lesbian members and their partners can stage a protest at the entrance of the student union and we will kiss during the prime hours of attendance. That will get their attention." Another student, Jasmine, isn't so sure about his idea. She replies, "I don't know, James. I'm just starting to come to terms with my sexuality. I don't think I'm ready for such a public display." The members of the group begin to debate the suggestion. Some are in favor of James's idea and others have serious reservations.

- What are the issues in this case?
- What are the organization's options for handling the situation? How might each option play out? Which option do you prefer?
- Why might some students like the idea and others be more hesitant? Would a student's stage of coming out affect his or her opinion of the idea?

- What are some other ways to get the organization recognized on campus?

## Everyone Has an Opinion

Amy is the president of the Jewish Student Organization. The organization is relatively small, only ten members. Amy lives with three other members of the organization. Because the four members live together, they occasionally hold impromptu meetings where they discuss the organization's upcoming events. Amy then attends a formal meeting with all the members and discusses what she and her roommates determined was best for the organization. This causes a problem within the organization. The other members resent that Amy and her roommates have made decisions without their input. Additionally, members are angered that Amy's boyfriend, Adam, although not an official member of the organization, often influences Amy by sharing his opinion of how the organization should run and what she should do.

As a whole, the organization decide that they want to increase their membership. They decide to send an electronic survey to all the Jewish students at the university to learn more about their needs as they relate to the organization. They send the survey to 150 Jewish students but receive only one response. The response comes from Adam. Most of his responses to the survey are ridiculous and many contain strong sexual overtones.

- What are the issues in this case?
- What are Amy's options for handling the issues? How might each option play out? Which option do you prefer?
- How should Amy handle her and her roommates' desire to strategize for the organization?
- How should Amy react to the lack of survey responses? Is there another way to increase participation among the Jewish students? How should Amy handle her boyfriend? What should she do if members of the organization are extremely offended by his responses but she doesn't think it is a big deal?

- Have you ever been part of an organization that you felt had a core group of individuals who made all the key decisions for the organization? How did you handle the problem?

## When a Co-president Is Disliked

Mercedes and Marisol are co-presidents of the Hispanic student organization. Although both women are dedicated to the organization, it quickly becomes apparent that the organization's advisor, Ricardo, doesn't like Mercedes. He schedules meetings with Marisol and doesn't invite Mercedes. When Marisol asks him about the oversight, he tells her that she can relay the information to Mercedes.

- What are the issues in this case?
- What are the options for handling the problem? How might each option play out? Which option do you prefer?
- What are the advantages and disadvantages of co-presidencies?
- How do you ensure effective communication when there are two people leading an organization?

## In Need of an Advisor

The GLBTQ Organization is in search of a new advisor. There are three people interested in serving in this capacity. Since the officers do not know all the prospective candidates, they decide to interview all of them. Mac, the president, notifies the three potential candidates of the interview. They become very angry because interviewing prospective advisors is a new process. The role of the advisor is a voluntary position and now three individuals are required to "compete" for the role. Since the organization tends to start meetings late, one candidate demands that the interviews be conducted on time. This same person then arrives fifteen minutes late for his interview. After the interviews, the group selects one advisor and notifies the others, who become very angry that they were not selected. The two candidates who were not chosen will not talk with the members of the organization and go out of their way to avoid them.

- What are the issues in this case?
- What are the organization's options for handling the situation? How might each option play out? Which option do you prefer?
- What do you think of the organization's strategy for selecting an advisor? Do you have any suggestions for how it might have handled things differently?
- Why do you think the potential advisors didn't like the selection process? Was there anything that could be done to make them feel more appreciated?

## Open to Anyone

An ethnic organization hosts a homecoming dance for students, alumni, and their friends. Basically the dance is open to anyone. Attendance is high, and the dance floor is full. Late in the evening a fight breaks out between two men attending the event. The men are not affiliated with the organization nor are they students or alumni of the university. Campus security is called and they arrive with their guns drawn.

- What are the issues in this case?
- If you were the president of the sponsoring organization, what would your options be for handling the situation? How might each option play out? Which option do you prefer?
- How might the organization have prevented the fight? What security measures are in place at your organization's events? How does your organization keep participants safe and the crowd controlled?
- What are your impressions of campus security showing up with guns drawn? Do you think this was appropriate? Why or why not? What would you do if campus security showed up with guns drawn at one of your organization's events? How might you address the situation with the director of campus security?

# A Bossy Advisor

Loretta, the advisor of the Black Student Union (BSU), is also an employee of the university that sponsors BSU. Part of her job assignment is to advise the group. She has advised BSU for the past eleven years. While the students appreciate her wisdom and years of experience, they also believe that she is very bossy. Rather than advise and guide the students, she tells them what to do. The students feel that their voices are not heard and that their ideas are not embraced. They have expressed their concerns to Loretta, but they feel that their concerns have fallen on deaf ears. Members of the organization are very frustrated and want Loretta removed as their advisor.

- What are the issues in this case?
- If you were the president of BSU, what would your options be for handling the situation? How might each option play out? Which option do you prefer?
- What might happen if you express your concerns to someone in a higher position than Loretta? What might be the impact?
- How do you communicate with your advisor? Do you have an open dialogue regarding your concerns with the organization? How might you build a stronger, more open relationship with your advisor?

# T-Shirts to Support National Coming Out Day

Christopher is the president of the Gay Straight Alliance (GSA) at Inandrus, a small, private liberal arts college that enrolls about 1,800 students. Although Christopher is heterosexual, he considers himself a gay ally. The GSA decides to purchase 600 T-shirts that say, "Gay, fine by me" to be worn by students on National Coming Out Day. The organization needs to raise $4,000 to buy the T-shirts. About half the members of the GSA want to be politically active and the others want to be more passive. The first fund-raising idea of the group is to collect soda can deposits. However, at 10 cents per can, collecting $4,000 worth of cans would take considerable time and effort. Christopher recognizes why the group opted for the safe and passive approach to fund-raising. He poses the pros and cons of the soda can fund-raising effort to the group and suggests that the members ask other student organizations for cosponsorship. He believes this is the most effective way to raise the funds in a short period of time. Since Christopher is heterosexual and comfortable with his sexual orientation, he recognizes that it may be easier for him to approach groups because it doesn't involve self-disclosure. He understands why it might be hard for some members to trust others when they have been discriminated against by them.

- What are the issues in this case?
- What are the group's options for handling the situation? How might each option play out? Which option do you prefer?
- What do you think of Christopher's suggestion? Should he take the lead in soliciting funds from other organizations?

## No More Room

Javier is the president of the Hispanic campus organization. The organization holds a dance on campus. The room can hold 200 individuals, and only about 125 are in attendance when the building manager tells Javier that no one else can come in. When Javier disagrees with him, the building manager calls campus security as a backup. Javier and members of the executive board are extremely frustrated because the event is under control and no one is causing a problem or a disturbance. Javier thinks that the building manager is overreacting because he is nervous about the number of Hispanics in the room.

- What are the issues in this case?
- What are Javier's options for handling the situation? How might each option play out? Which option do you prefer?
- How might Javier and the executive board prevent something like this from happening again? Do you have any suggestions for how they should have handled the situation differently? What would you do if you were Javier?

## Day of Silence

As part of Gay Pride Week, all students who support the GLBTQ campus community are asked to observe a day of silence. Those who are participating wear a button in support of the cause and also give their faculty a note explaining why they are not speaking in class on that day. Most faculty members understand and support the students' decisions to be silent. Dr. Jones, a boisterous faculty member in the psychology department, does not understand. Prior to the day of silence, Dr. Jones makes some subtle homophobic comments in class. At the beginning of his psychology 101 course, five students approach him with their notes explaining why they will be silent in class. Dr. Jones reads the notes, gives them back to the students, and then announces that anyone who chooses not to actively participate in that day's class will have his or her grade lowered by half a letter grade. The students are shocked and angered by Dr. Jones's response. Not wanting their grades to drop, they speak in class. After the class ends they find Betty, the president of the GLBTQ Organization, and inform her of Dr. Jones's response and request that the group do something about him and his homophobic ways.

- What are the issues in this case?
- What are Betty's options for handling the situation? How might each option play out? Which option do you prefer?
- Are there procedures on your campus for reporting inappropriate comments? Should the students have reported Dr. Jones the day before the day of silence, when he made inappropriate comments? Why or why not? Should he be reported for not supporting the day of silence? Why or why not?

## Recruiting White Supremacists

A local neo-Nazi group is on campus speaking and trying to recruit members. Although the campus administration does not support the group being on campus, the white supremacists are sponsored by a faculty member. The university is not happy about them being on campus, but it cannot limit their right to free speech. The group registered its demonstration and was given the university protest guidelines, which it followed.

Students of color, in particular, are outraged. They believe the university is supporting the neo-Nazis and not them. At the end of the demonstration, campus police even escort the neo-Nazis to their cars. The students are angered that campus police are protecting them. The chief of police releases a statement the next day informing the campus community that his officers were not protecting the demonstrators or showing any support for their topic. The officers were actually escorting them to their cars to ensure their prompt departure from the campus.

- What are the issues in this case?
- What are the options for handling the situation? How might each option play out? Which option do you prefer?
- What do you think of the way that the university handled the situation? What did it do right and wrong? What suggestions would you have for handling a similar situation in the future?
- What message was the university sending to its students by hosting this group on campus? Given that the university cannot limit someone's right to free speech, could it have done anything different?
- As a student leader, what is your obligation in addressing the anger of students? How might you understand the situation more fully and communicate the administration's action to your peers?

## Dressing Up

You recently learn that at the annual Halloween party for Sigma Tri Delta fraternity two of the members attended the party in blackface, and two other members accompanied them dressed as members of the Ku Klux Klan. You decide to look up some of the members on Facebook to learn more about the event. You are shocked to see that two of the members posted pictures of themselves dressed as Klansmen. As the president of the African American Student Coalition, you are outraged, as are the other members of the coalition. You bring this problem to the attention of the dean of students. He says that he will look into the situation but that it will be very difficult to do anything because your college is a state university where free speech is protected.

- What are the issues in this case?
- What are your options for handling the situation? How might each option play out? Which option do you prefer?

- What are your impressions of the dean's response? How does one respect freedom of speech while denouncing blatant racism?
- What actions do you recommend that the university take and why?

# No Representation

Every year your university selects five outstanding male and five outstanding female student leaders as homecoming ambassadors. On some campuses, these ambassadors may also be known as the homecoming court. Each student organization may nominate one male and one female. Those nominated put together portfolios detailing their leadership experiences, academic performance, and commitment to service learning. A committee of students, faculty, and staff reviews the portfolios, interviews the candidates, and selects the ten homecoming ambassadors. From these ten men and women, the student body elects a king and a queen. In the past two years, there has not been a person of color recognized as a homecoming ambassador. This frustrates the members of the ethnic student organizations because they believe that they nominate top students but that these students are not selected because of their minority status.

- What are the issues in this case?
- If you were a leader of one of the minority student organizations, what would your options be for handling this situation? How might each option play out? Which option do you prefer?
- Whom should you talk with regarding your concerns? If there are persons of color represented on the selection committee, should you talk with them? Should you just forget what happened and hope that the committee will select your candidate next year?
- In general, how do you decide which battles to fight?

# Planning Pride Week

Gay, lesbian, bisexual, and transgender (GLBTQ) pride week is planned by a joint committee of faculty, administrators, and students. Gilbert, the new and somewhat inexperienced director of the GLBTQ office, coordinates the effort. His supervisor tells him who will serve on the planning committee. Gilbert quickly contacts the names on the list and holds the first meeting of the planning committee. Right from the beginning, the two faculty members and the two students from the GLBTQ Organization start arguing about the events. There is obvious disagreement about the events that should be planned, who should coordinate them, and whose week this really is. After the meeting, the two faculty members approach Gilbert and ask him to limit the students' involvement. They tell him that the students are inexperienced, horrible with follow-through, and not thinking about the entire campus community. Giving in to the faculty members' suggestion, Gilbert limits the students' involvement. The students know that Gilbert is being bullied by the two faculty members, and although they are frustrated, they don't blame him for the situation. The students decide to limit their involvement, and as a result, student attendance at the pride events is low.

- What are the issues in this case?
- What are the options for handling the situation? How might each option play out? Which option do you prefer?
- If you were one of the two students who were asked to limit their involvement, would you?
- Should you respect the wishes of your advisor in this case?
- Would you discourage students from participating in the pride week events? What would be the pros and cons of doing so?
- How would you ensure that student voices are represented in the planning of pride week for next year?

## Fraternity Recruitment

Your friend Lashawn, who is active in the Black Student Association, informs you that he is interested in joining a Greek organization. You are excited because you are the chapter president of one of the historically Black fraternities and you would love to recruit him. A couple of weeks go by and you learn that your friend joined a historically White fraternity. You are shocked and angry.

- What are the issues in this case?
- What are your options for handling the situation? How might each option play out? Which option do you prefer?
- Why do you think you are angry that Lashawn joined a traditionally White fraternity?
- Do you think African Americans should join only historically Black fraternities and Whites only historically White fraternities? Why or why not?

# Ghetto Fabulous Party

You are the president of one of the multicultural organizations on campus, and one of the members brings to your attention that a campus organization sponsored an end-of-year party with a "Ghetto Fabulous" theme. All of the partygoers dressed in exaggerated hip-hop clothing. They played hip-hop music and tried to talk and dance "ghetto." Members of your organization found out about the event when individuals planning to attend asked if they could borrow some of their clothing.

- What are the issues in this case?
- What are your options for handling the situation? How might each option play out? Which option do you prefer?
- Why do you think the members of the organization were offended by the requests to borrow their clothing? How should they have responded to the requests? Why?

# Where Did the New Members Go?

Each fall approximately 100 members attend the first meeting of the Gay Straight Alliance (GSA). Typically, members of the executive board are very extroverted, have come out about their sexuality, and have an activist agenda. This overwhelms some of the newcomers who attend the first meeting because they are just coming to terms with their sexuality. Because many are intimidated by the perceived activist agenda, they do not attend any additional meetings.

Claire is very nervous about attending her first meeting. Since she has only recently decided that she is bisexual, she is really worried about how she will be perceived by the group. She attends the meeting in the hopes of finding a support group and some new compassionate friends. As the meeting starts, she is immediately turned off because one of the executive board members is bad-mouthing a fellow gay student who happens to be one of Claire's friends. This, in addition to the intimidating activist agenda, sends Claire fleeing from the meeting swearing that she will never attend another one.

- What are the issues in this case?
- What are Claire's options for handling the situation? How might each option play out? Which option do you prefer?
- If you were president of the organization and you saw a drop in attendance from 100 members at the first meeting to 50 at the second and 30 at the third, what would that tell you? How could you better address the needs of your constituents?
- What advice do you have for Claire? What advice do you have for the leaders of the GSA?

# Anti–Gay Pride Week

Sonia is the president of a religious organization. On tonight's meeting agenda is the topic of Gay Pride Week. A debate ensues over the organization's potential participation in sponsoring anti-gay events during this week. Half of the members of the organization want to sponsor anti-gay religious programs so that people will be informed about the church's stance on homosexuality. They want to write letters to the editor of the school paper, host debates so that the campus community will learn from opposing views, sponsor a controversial anti-gay speaker, and possibly hold a protest. The rest of the members don't want to do anything during that week and believe that the organization should respect the GLBTQ students' programs and events. These members will not participate in or condone the proposed anti-gay events. Sonia is very confused and doesn't know what to do. She personally believes that homosexuality is a sin, but she wants to respect all members of her organization.

- What are the issues in this case?
- What are Sonia's options for handling the situation? How might each option play out? Which option do you prefer?
- As a student leader, can you make all members of your organization happy? Why or why not?
- Have you ever been in a situation in which your personal beliefs contradicted the sentiments of your organization? How did you handle this problem? Have you ever had another student leader try to impose his or her beliefs on the organization? If so, what was the group's reaction?

## Count Off

Carlos is the president of a multicultural student organization. Each year the group holds an end-of-semester dance/party at a venue off campus. The owner of the club where the event is to be held this year informs Carlos that he will have to provide him with an accurate head count. Carlos tells the owner that 150 students will be in attendance.

On the night of the party, more people start to show up as the evening progresses. Most are uninvited and unexpected. Carlos is having such a good time that he doesn't really notice. In the meantime, the owner grows more and more frustrated. At 11:00 P.M., the owner turns on the lights and makes everyone line up against the wall for a head count. Many members of the organization are outraged by this demand and claim that he purposefully disrupted the party because the majority of the attendees are African American.

- What are the issues in this case?
- What are Carlos's options for handling the situation? How might each option play out? Which option do you prefer?
- Was the owner's action justified? What do you think should happen if the head count revealed that the number of guests exceeded the

club's capacity? What do you think would have happened if a fight broke out?

- How do you currently extend invitations to your events? Do you prepare a guest list? Do people sign in? Do they have to be students at the university or guests of a member? What are the pros and cons of limiting the guest list?

## Asian American Pride Week

In preparing for Asian American Pride Week, the multicultural student center asks the Asian American Student Organization to put in a funding request to help offset the cost of most of the events. Only student organizations can request money from the student activity fee, so this is why the center has asked your group to put in the request; however, its office will plan the events. As president of the Asian American Student Organization, you know that the university gives the multicultural center funding for the week, so you are not sure why the center needs the additional money. You feel very conflicted because you want as many events during this week as possible but you are concerned about the actions of the administrators in the multicultural student center.

- What are the issues in this case?
- What are your options for handling the situation? How might each option play out? Which option do you prefer?
- If you were told that without the additional money there would be no Asian American Pride Week, what would you do?
- Has your organization ever been asked to request student activity funds to pay for campuswide events? If so, how did you handle such a request? Do you think the request was appropriate?

# 7

# ORIENTATION/WELCOME
# WEEK CASES

## Racist Comments at Northern Community College

Your role as a student ambassador at Northern Community College is to help students find classes during the first weeks of the quarter and organize and staff a welcome table to assist students. The Monday after the first week is slow, because most students have found their classrooms and seem to be settling into a routine. You are about ready to leave an academic building to get to class when you hear yelling from down the hall. As you walk down the hall, you see an apparently irritated person who is yelling racial obscenities. Unsure of whether the person is a student, you approach him. This causes the person to yell even louder. You become frightened because you don't know if this person is capable of physical harm.

- What are the issues in this case?
- What are your options for handling the situation? How might each option play out? Which option do you prefer?
- What is the first thing you should do as you approach the student and realize his apparent distress? Should you continue to approach the student alone or leave to get assistance?
- How would you use this situation to open discussions about and initiate programming for diversity and tolerance training? Who would facilitate the discussions and programming?

*123*

## Are You Really Sick?

Your orientation/registration program for new students takes place over the course of two days and one night. For many first-year students, this is the first time they are away from home and they are "eager" to experience college for the first time. Although they are excited to be on campus, many don't want the orientation experience. They prefer to drink and party rather than attend the prescribed orientation events. Students are notified in writing prior to orientation and then reminded by their orientation leaders that they may not leave campus.

At about midnight, Sue, one of the orientation leaders, is approached by Liv, a new student. Liv claims that she fell out of bed and wants to leave. Rather than allow the student to leave the orientation program, Sue insists that she transport Liv to the local urgent care facility. Despite Liv's resistance, Sue transports her. The doctor finds nothing wrong and sends her back to orientation. A couple of days after orientation, Sue checks Liv's Facebook account and learns about how Liv hated orientation and how she tried to "fake" her way out of it.

- What are the issues in this case?
- What are the options for handling the situation? How might each option play out? Which option do you prefer?
- What is your assessment of the orientation leader's response? What were her options for handling the new student's accident? What would be the consequences if she had refused to let the student leave and hadn't had the resident take her to the hospital, and the student's condition had worsened?
- What is your campus policy regarding hospital/urgent care transports? Should an orientation leader transport a student individually or should he or she take another leader with him or her? What are the pros and cons of having one versus two escorts?
- Should anything be done as a result of the student's Facebook comments? Should the leader respond personally? Should the leader tell the orientation director? Should the leader just let it go since her orientation session is over and it's no longer her problem?

- Do you discuss Facebook, MySpace, and other online blogging with your orientation group? Why might it be important to discuss public access to these sites?

# FYE Instructor

Yuki is a peer mentor for the Freshman Year Experience (FYE) at Hoptown University (HU). One of her responsibilities is to cofacilitate a freshman seminar with Dr. Linda Jackson, a sociology professor at HU. During the week before classes the FYE program has an orientation for all course facilitators. Yuki is excited because she has never met Dr. Jackson. The orientation is extremely productive for Yuki except for the fact that Dr. Jackson does not show up. This makes Yuki anxious, because it is now Thursday and their first class meeting is Monday.

Yuki sends Dr. Jackson an e-mail Thursday night and does not hear back by Friday afternoon. She calls her office and also stops by with no success. On Sunday morning, Dr. Jackson returns Yuki's e-mail and asks her to think about the kinds of things she would like to see done during the semester. In addition, she asks Yuki to come to class a little early so they can discuss their plan. Yuki spends the next few hours making an outline of what she would like to do this semester and see covered in the course.

On Monday, Yuki arrives at the classroom a half hour early to meet with Dr. Jackson. Dr. Jackson arrives fifteen minutes later and immediately asks Yuki for the syllabus. Yuki is confused and says she worked on some goals and activities, but not a formal syllabus. Dr. Jackson says that this is unacceptable and that they need to get things straight if this peer-mentoring relationship is going to work this semester.

Dr. Jackson conducts the class session and does all the facilitating. She waits until the very end to introduce Yuki. As the semester goes on Dr. Jackson gives Yuki all the responsibility for preparation and grading, but she does not invite Yuki to facilitate discussions or class activities. Yuki is extremely frustrated with Dr. Jackson and the experience. She discusses the situation with her roommate and decides that she is going to talk with the director of the FYE program.

The director seems surprised to hear of Yuki's situation. She asks Yuki if she has talked to Dr. Jackson. Yuki tells her that she hasn't, because she isn't sure that would be a good idea. The director then gets a bit upset and tells Yuki that she needs to do that first. She goes on to say that as a student leader Yuki should know the appropriate protocol.

- What are the issues in this case?
- What are Yuki's options for handling the situation? How might each option play out? Which option do you prefer?
- What should Yuki do now? How should Yuki approach Dr. Jackson?
- Are there other individuals or offices Yuki should include in the conversation with Dr. Jackson?
- What are the major issues that FYE training should address to help peer mentors avoid situations like this?

## Smoking Pot at Orientation

Freshman orientation is a time to meet new people, tour campus, register for classes, and get a feel for how your freshman year may proceed. Tom and Jack arrive at freshman orientation "bright eyed and bushy tailed" and ready to begin the process of becoming official students at Middle Mountain University (MMU). Both were excellent students in high school and Tom even plans to try out for the university lacrosse team.

Orientation begins with some icebreakers. After that, students are split off with orientation leaders based on housing assignments. Since Tom and Jack are living together they are in the same group. Luke is their orientation leader. He is going to be a junior English major at MMU and is excited to work with this group of new students. Luke leads the group back to the hall where they will be staying for the evening and tells the students that they have an hour or so to hang out before the next scheduled events. He tells them that they should not go too far, because MMU is a huge campus and it is easy to get lost. Tom and Jack decide to stay in their residence hall room, because they don't have that much time to explore.

After hanging out for a while, they hear laughter and music coming from the third room down from theirs. They decide to venture down and see what is going on. Once there, they knock on the door. Luke answers but only opens the door halfway. Tom asks if they can join the party because they are bored. Luke closes the door. A few moments later he reopens it and invites the two into the room but only if they say they can keep a secret. Inside the room five male students are smoking marijuana. Tom and Jack are pretty surprised and feel extremely uncomfortable. All Tom can think about is the introduction from the orientation director. She made it very clear that participating in illegal activities or not following curfew at orientation would lead to immediate expulsion from MMU.

Tom looks at Jack and motions for the door. They decide that they should leave before either one is tempted to participate. Luke comes over to them and asks if they would like a few hits. Both say no and that they should be going. As Jack and Tom are leaving the room, Cindy, the head student orientation counselor, comes down the hall and confronts them. She announces, "You are not going anywhere, and neither is anyone else in this room."

- What are the issues in this case? What are the issues involving the orientation leader? Involving Tom and Jack?
- What are the options for handling the orientation leader? For handling Tom and Jack? How might each option play out? Which option do you prefer?
- Should Jack and Tom be held responsible? How should Luke and the other men in the room be sanctioned?
- Should Luke be more responsible because of his role as an orientation leader? Should he be allowed to keep his job?
- Do you know of times when orientation leaders break the rules? What message does this send to new students? How might you prevent something like what Luke did from happening? Do you have clear expectations for your orientation leaders? Do you have clear consequences if someone breaks a rule or policy?

## My Parents Won't Let Go

You are an orientation leader assigned to parent orientation. One of the parents in particular appears very distraught that she cannot participate in her daughter's orientation. She would rather go through the student orientation with her daughter than attend the parent program. She approaches you, concerned that her daughter won't know which classes to take or won't wake up in time to register. She has a list of reasons why she needs to be with her daughter during the two-day orientation program.

- What are the issues in this case?
- What are your options for handling the situation? How might each option play out? Which option do you prefer?
- What would you say to the student's mother to make her feel more comfortable about her daughter going through the orientation without her help?
- Why might it be difficult for some parents to let their children experience orientation on their own? How might you help parents start to see their children as independent adults? How might you help students see themselves as independent adults?

## Ice Cream, Anyone?

During a break from student orientation events, four new students decide to walk a block off campus to get ice cream. While at the ice cream parlor, they meet two upper-class students who invite them to a keg party later that evening. Two of the students decide to leave the orientation social early to attend the party. Their orientation leader finds out and notifies the orientation director, who notifies the dean of students. Their acceptance to the university is withdrawn.

- What are the issues in this case?
- What are the options for handling the situation? How might each option play out? Which option do you prefer?
- Should the orientation leader have told the director about the students? If the students had been informed at the beginning of orientation that they must attend all orientation events and that drinking alcohol during orientation could result in rescinding of their admission, would the orientation leader be justified in telling on them?
- Do you think rescinding their admission was an appropriate response for their behavior? How should they be treated if they had skipped other orientation events?

# Inappropriate Advances

Romy is an orientation leader at Spy College in upstate New York. She has worked with the summer orientation program for two years and is excited to have more of a leadership role this summer. She has met many full-time campus employees during the two years and also a number of other students from across campus.

Dirk, her favorite custodian, has worked at Spy College for ten years. He works in the halls that host the summer orientation program. Over the past couple of summers, Romy has gone out of her way to be nice to Dirk, and the two have had some interesting conversations. During orientation, Romy decides to take Dirk some cookies because she has not seen him much as she is living in an off-campus house. She heard through the grapevine that Dirk lost his life partner during the winter, so she thought maybe he could use a pick-me-up.

Romy finds Dirk in the laundry room of Toast Hall. He is cleaning the dryer filters. Unaware that she is there, he is startled when she approaches him. She apologizes and says, "I just wanted to bring you some cookies I made last night." He is really excited to see Romy and walks over to give her a hug. The two sit on top of the washers to chat for a bit. When Romy asks Dirk about his loss, he becomes very despondent and distant. She gets off the washer to make eye contact. While she is looking into his eyes, Dirk jumps down and embraces her. At first Romy doesn't think anything of his embrace. After a few moments, though, she tries to free herself, but Dirk will not let her go. He says, "You feel so good I could hold on to you forever. I like this." Romy gets worried and begins feeling a bit claustrophobic in the laundry room. She says, "Dirk, I have to be going now." He suddenly pulls away and says, "You cannot come down here with cookies and come on to me and then just walk away, you little tease." Romy is now really frightened and runs out of the room.

When Romy gets back upstairs, she immediately runs to the orientation office. Since it is late in the evening, the only person in the office is a colleague named Jonah. Romy doesn't know him well but has to tell someone about what has happened. She tells him the whole story and asks what she should do. Jonah says, "You need to report this to Beth, the director of orientation. He is in the wrong, not you." Romy replies, "I know, but after all, I did go down there. Maybe I gave him the wrong impression."

- What are the issues in this case?
- What are Romy's options for handling the situation? How might each option play out? Which option do you prefer?

## Community Relations

You are a student and an orientation leader at Evans College, a small, private liberal arts college in the city of Marian. Evans College tends to recruit predominantly White students from middle- to upper-class backgrounds. Although Evans College attracts affluent students, the surrounding community has lost various industries in the past two decades. As a result, Marian's economy is struggling. The community of Marian is predominantly African American and most inhabitants are of low to middle socioeconomic status. There has always been conflict between the residents of Marian and the students of Evans College. Although the college and community leaders work well together, many from the Marian community believe that the Evans students are spoiled White kids.

During orientation, two Evans students decide to walk downtown. Both students are White and have had little exposure to persons of color. Halfway to town, a car with three African American teenagers from the community in it approaches, the car slows down, and the three yell out, "Spoiled White kids. Why don't you go back to your rich mommies and daddies? You aren't wanted here." The car then speeds away. The Evans students are shaken by the incident as they recount it to you, their orientation leader. They plan to call their parents. They had asked about relations with the community on their campus tour and had been assured that they would not encounter any problems with members of the community. They are scared and talking about switching schools.

- What are the issues in this case?
- What are your options for handling the situation? How might each option play out? Which option do you prefer?
- Should you be honest and tell the students that relations between the residents and students are strained and risk potentially losing the students? Should you talk with the students about ways to get involved in the community? Should you challenge the students to learn from the incident?

- What would you do if the students were women and they were concerned about their physical safety?
- How are the relations between your college/university and members of the surrounding community? What is the community's opinion of your college? Is that opinion warranted? What might your school do to improve community relations?

## Orientation Skit

Every year the orientation team plans an initial skit for the start of orientation week. The team members prepare the skit in case they are running ahead of schedule and need to fill time by entertaining the new students, but they are never sure they will actually use it.

It is the second night of orientation and the opening speaker is late, so at the very last minute the senior orientation leaders decide to have the orientation leaders perform the skit. Because of the last-minute decision, two orientation leaders don't get the message about the addition to the program. When they see the others on stage performing, they get very upset and jump to the conclusion that they were purposely left out. They are so upset that they get in one of the university vans and leave campus at 7:00 P.M. Around 9:00 P.M., one of the new students gets sick and needs to go to an after-hours medical care facility, but there is no van to transport her. The two leaders are still gone with the van and are nowhere to be found. Other leaders try calling them on their cell phones but get no response. A group of orientation leaders even go out in their personal cars looking for the two disgruntled leaders but cannot find them. The two finally return to campus around 11:00 P.M., and the rest of the team is very angry. The two disgruntled leaders are also still very angry.

- What are the issues in this case?
- If you were a senior orientation leader, what would your options be for handling the situation? Which option do you prefer?
- How would you handle the two leaders who left? Are their feelings a factor? Why do you think they reacted the way that they did?
- How would you rebuild your orientation team? How would you handle future communications in order to prevent future misunderstandings? How would you encourage the staff not to jump to conclusions?

- Have you ever had a problem with miscommunication that resulted in confusion or hurt feelings? How did you handle the situation?

## Scavenger Hunt

Two senior orientation leaders, Juan and Rose, are in charge of planning an informative campus scavenger hunt for the new orientation leaders. The purpose of the scavenger hunt is to do something fun that also orients new leaders to various resources on campus. In past years, the hunt has also been a great team-building activity.

Juan and Rose spend a great deal of time coordinating the hunt. To their surprise, while participating in the event, most of the new orientation leaders complain. They don't want to run or walk to the various places on campus. They think the hunt is dumb and are not shy about expressing their dissatisfaction the entire time. By the time the new leaders arrive at their final location, Juan and Rose are very angry, because they tried to do something fun for the new leaders and all they did was complain. They fear that the negative attitudes will impact the entire orientation process.

- What are the issues in this case?
- What are Juan and Rose's options for handling the situation? Which option do you prefer?
- What are your suggestions for improving morale?
- Have you ever been in a group that had a few negative members who tended to influence the rest of the group? How did you handle the situation?
- Should the senior orientation leaders hold the scavenger hunt next year? Are there any other ways that they could orient the new leaders to campus?

## First Impressions

The first issue of the campus newspaper is available on freshman move-in day. One of the articles calls freshmen "easy meat" and encourages them to get drunk and be promiscuous. Upperclassmen know that the paper does this every year for "shock" value. This year it certainly provokes a response. A few of the parents read the paper, become outraged, and come to you demanding an explanation.

- What are the issues in this case?
- What are your possible responses to the parents? Which response do you prefer?
- Who should receive the feedback regarding the negative response?
- Is there anything that can be done to prevent this type of article from being published in the future?
- Is your school a public or private one? How does this factor into freedom-of-speech issues?

## Orientation Leader Bias

Camilla, one of the orientation leaders, is antifraternity and antisorority. Over the course of orientation, it becomes evident that she is using her position as an orientation leader to encourage new students *not* to go through formal recruitment. She tells new students that fraternities and sororities "buy their friends, haze, and are all a bunch of sloppy drunks." Some of the new students who are interested in joining a fraternity or sorority tell two of the other orientation leaders who are members. They become outraged and plan to confront Camilla.

- What are the issues in this case?
- If you were the senior orientation leader, what would your options be for handling the situation? How might each option play out? Which option do you prefer?
- If the two Greek orientation leaders were promoting the Greek system, would their anger be justified?
- If Camilla wasn't anti-Greek but was very religious and using her Christian beliefs to sway the new students, would her actions be justified?
- Is it okay for orientation leaders to use their beliefs or values to influence new students? If you believe that all students should get involved

in student organizations, would it be okay to encourage them to get involved? Where do you draw the line when it comes to using your influence?

## Hometown Boys

Four male students attending your orientation session are all from the same hometown. They have an "I'm too cool for orientation" attitude. They are not interested in being at orientation. They crack jokes throughout the session and do not pay attention to the speakers. When you ask them to respect others and the orientation process, they respond with more arrogance.

- What are the issues in this case?
- What are your options for handling the situation? How might each option play out? Which option do you prefer?
- Have you ever had a situation in which a student wasn't willing to listen? Did his or her attitude distract the rest of the group? In such a situation, what would you do if other new students started to mimic the problem student's actions? How would you keep control of the group?

## Attention Seeker

Derek, one of the new students in your orientation group, tells you he is gay. One day, he decides to tell the rest of the members of the group. They are very supportive. Over the course of the day, Derek continues to direct the group's attention toward him. He shares that his parents are divorced, that he had problems with peers in high school, and that he was sexually abused as a child. While members of the orientation group try to be supportive, they start to perceive him as an attention seeker. His stories start to bring down the group. As Derek's orientation leader, you want to support him and validate his feelings but you also realize how his admissions are impacting the group dynamics. Feelings start to escalate and the group's animosity starts to break down the group dynamics.

- What are the issues in this case?
- What are your options for handling the situation? How might each option play out? Which option do you prefer?
- Do you have one strategy for Derek and another for the orientation group?
- Should you talk about the issue as a group or should you talk with Derek alone? What should you say to Derek?
- What do you think is at the root of the group's conflict? Could it be that the others are frustrated that they only get to hear from Derek and don't have the opportunity to talk? Should you allow the others an opportunity to talk?

# Blame Game

Intentionally, your school invites controversial orientation speakers to campus. It does this so that the orientation groups can engage in a thoughtful discussion surrounding the issues. Past controversial topics have included abortion, affirmative action in college admissions, and various political debates. This year's orientation speaker is especially controversial. She is supposed to discuss racism, but at one point in her speech she mentions that a family member was raped. The speaker goes on to say that the rape was partially the victim's fault because she was intoxicated and found herself in an inappropriate situation. After the speaker, you convene your orientation group to discuss the topics presented by the speaker. The group quickly starts to debate whether or not rape is the victim's fault. Marisa, a new student, insists that if a woman is raped, it is partially her fault. Two other women in the group become quite upset and start to cry. Eventually, both admit that they are victims of rape.

- What are the issues in this case?
- What are your options for handling the situation? How might each option play out? Which option do you prefer?
- Is rape ever the victim's fault?
- What suggestions do you have regarding safety on campus? What recommendations do you have for rape prevention? What resources are available on your campus to help victims of sexual assault and rape?

- What suggestions do you have for men to help them avoid being accused of rape?
- What is your campus procedure for reporting acts of sexual aggression?

# Rate a Professor

Part of your role as the orientation leader is to assist students with their fall schedules. Although you are advised not to give students advice on professors, one of the new students brings up one of the many Websites where students can rate their professors. She asks you what your opinion of these sites is and whether or not the students can access them in designing their schedules.

- What are the issues in this case?
- How should you respond? What should you do if all of the students in the orientation group are eager to learn more about these Websites?
- If you are specifically instructed by the orientation director not to allow students to access these sites but you personally have used them to choose classes, what should you do?

# Scheduling to Party

When choosing classes, one of the new students says to you, "I was told that I shouldn't schedule any classes on Fridays because everyone parties on Thursday night or goes home on Fridays. What do you think? I was also told never to take a class before 10:00 A.M. because the residence halls get pretty loud late into the night. Is that a good idea?"

- What are the issues in this case?
- What are your options for handling the situation? How might each option play out? Which option do you prefer?
- If at your school Thursday night is a big party night but you've been informed by your orientation leader not to promote partying, should you be honest with the student?

## One Leader or Two?

At Yanger University two orientation leaders are assigned to each group of twelve new students. Michelle and Amed are assigned to the same group. They are paired together throughout orientation. Both are first-year orientation leaders and eager to meet and help the new students. Soon after their first meeting with the new students, it becomes apparent that Michelle likes to talk. Her desire to talk is related partly to her enthusiasm about being an orientation leader and partly to her eagerness to share all that she knows about Yanger with the new students. At times Amed tries to add his input but Michelle quickly cuts him off. She dominates the conversations and soon the members of the group start to gravitate toward her. They direct their questions to her and they start to see her as the "expert"; they ignore Amed. Amed is getting more and more frustrated.

- What are the issues in this case?
- What are Amed's options for handling the situation? How might each option play out? Which option do you prefer?
- How might Amed perceive Michelle's behavior? Why might he think she is cutting him off and dominating the conversation?
- How might Michelle perceive Amed's behavior? Why might she think that he isn't speaking?
- Have you ever been part of a group with cofacilitators? Was there a tendency for one to dominate the conversation? If so, how did that impact the group dynamics? Why do you think one facilitator talked more than the other?

## A Diverse Applicant Pool?

You are one of two senior orientation leaders in charge of leader selection for next year. You notice that of the 100 applicants for 60 orientation leader spots, there are only 8 students of color. This concerns you a great deal, because chances are all 8 will not be hired. Diversification of the orientation leader staff is essential, because only 20 percent of the incoming freshman class are students of color. The deadline for applications is past due. This is the second year in a row that you have had such a low turnout of students of color.

- What are the issues in this case?
- What are your options for handling the situation? How might each option play out? Which option do you prefer?
- If the director of orientation insists that the applicant pool better reflect the diversity of the student body, what are your options?
- Why do you think this problem has happened two years in a row? What could be done to recruit more students of color?
- Do you think it is important to have students of color on the orientation staff? Why or why not?

## Partying and Breaking Curfew before School Begins

Emilia and Honey are two new freshmen at Willow University. They are on campus for orientation, and to say they are excited is an understatement. Both are first-generation college students from a small town four hours from campus. Emilia's mother drove them to campus but decided not to stay for parent orientation.

The two women decide to room with different people so they can meet other freshmen. Emilia is rooming with a woman from England, and Honey is staying with a woman who lives in the same town as the university. Both like their short-term roommates and are enjoying the first day of orientation.

The first day ends with a campus bus tour. During the bus tour, the group gets a good view of Reedville, where Willow is located. It is a big city that houses two other universities. Downtown is on the west side of Willow, and many junior and senior students opt to live in residences along that side. In addition, all the fraternity and sorority houses are located on the west side of the campus.

During the barbeque outside the residence hall where the students are staying for the orientation, Emilia, Honey, and their roommates meet Patti. She is the president of the Gamma sorority. She begins telling the four women about the sorority and the benefits of the Greek system at Willow. As she ends the conversation, she gives the women a flyer for a party that the chapter is sponsoring that evening. The flyer is designed for orientation students and talks about beach volleyball. The women are excited about the party as they head back to their room.

Back in their room, the women discuss what they want to do that evening. Honey says, "We really shouldn't go to the party. We are not supposed to leave campus during orientation." Diana, the woman from England, replies, "So what? How would anyone find out? Plus, it's something affiliated with campus and it's very close to campus." Then she adds, "And if it weren't allowed Patti wouldn't have been at the barbeque inviting orientation students." Emilia chimes in, "Well, we can check it out and see what we think, and if it's no good or we have a bad feeling about it we can leave."

The four women get ready and then head over to the party. They are greeted by Patti and a number of other Gamma sisters when they arrive. The atmosphere is lighthearted and fun. As she looks around, Emilia realizes that many of the sisters as well as a number of the orientation students and leaders are drinking. The four decide it would be okay to have a few drinks themselves. Emilia finds out later that Patti is an orientation leader, in addition to being president of the sorority. The women decide around midnight that it is time to leave the party. They are well past curfew and if they do not want to get into trouble they need to get back to their hall. On the way back, they run into Michael, an orientation leader in charge of nightly rounds. He asks where they have been. All four women look at each other and no one answers. He asks them again where they have been. Honey knows that if they tell, all the people at the party will probably get into trouble. She also knows that the four of them may get into trouble. She decides not to say anything, so Michael takes all their names and tells them to get back to their rooms and report to the orientation office by 8 A.M. As they continue walking back to their room, they discuss what may happen in the morning. They could all face expulsion from Willow.

- What are the issues in this case?
- What are the options for handling the situation? How might each option play out? Which option do you prefer?
- Should the four women get into trouble? If so, how severe should the punishment be?
- Do you think the four women should report Patti and the other orientation leaders? Why or why not? If they should, how should the university handle their actions?

- In what ways does Patti use her leadership roles to encourage poor choices by the students at orientation?

# My Online Stalker

During orientation Clarice meets another first-year student, Chase. The next day she decides to check him out on one of the social network Websites. Based on his groups, they have many similar interests. She decides to e-mail him. He quickly responds and joins her group of friends. They start corresponding via the Website and eventually decide to meet for a cup of coffee. The initial date goes well, but Clarice feels no romantic chemistry. She continues to e-mail Chase but declines his invitation for another date. Chase is upset and demands to see her so that she can explain why she doesn't want to date him anymore. At that point, Clarice stops communicating with Chase. Since she has her schedule online, it's easy for Chase to know where to find her. He starts popping up outside her classrooms, at the library, and outside her residence hall room. Clarice tells him to stop following her and that she isn't interested, but that only seems to make Chase pursue her more. Clarice is angry and a little scared. She comes to you for advice. She wants him banned from the building.

- What are the issues in this case?
- What are your options for handling the situation? How might each option play out? Which option do you prefer?
- At what point does campus security need to be informed?
- What precautions do you recommend that Clarice take to protect herself?
- If Chase is a resident in your building, what should you do?

# 8

# ACTIVITIES/PROGRAMMING BOARD AND FEE ALLOCATION CASES

## Padding the Budget

S tudent organization funding is very controversial on your campus. Student organizations typically request about 10 times the amount of available funds. This makes the job of the allocation committee very difficult because it is unable to fund many worthwhile programs. Over time it has become well known among the student organizations that they need to excessively pad their budget requests, because most organizations, regardless of the quality of the proposed events, receive only about 5 to 10 percent of the requested amount. Although some student organizations use the "padding" technique, others have completely lost faith in the funding process and do not even file funding requests because they do not think it is worth their time given the minimal amount of money that they receive.

- What are the issues in this case?
- What are the options for handling the situation? How might each option play out? Which option do you prefer?

- How should the allocation board address the perceptions of the allocation process?
- How is the allocation process viewed on your campus? Do student organizations manipulate the funding process on your campus? How?
- How do you make decisions about funding, especially given limited funding? Do you give a straight percentage or do you evaluate the quality of each program? How do you allocate fairly?

# Who Should Be Funded?

The student fee allocation committee receives two requests for funding. The first is submitted by the Korean student organization. It wants $1,000 for a party/cultural event. The committee knows that only 15 to 20 people will attend. At the same time, the committee receives another request from a predominantly White group for a speaker and reception. It knows that this event will be attended by approximately 200 White students. The committee has only $1,000 to allocate. However, both groups have made it clear that they need the full $1,000 to host their event and that if they are not awarded the full funding, they will not host the event.

- What are the issues in this case?
- What are the committee's options for handling the situation? How might each option play out? Which option do you prefer?
- If the campus is predominantly White, should the committee award funding only to the event that reaches the most people?
- If the campus is trying to do more to retain minority students and there has been a recent outcry regarding the lack of diversity in programming on campus, how should the committee allocate the funds?

# Appropriate Spending

The student fee allocation process on your campus is extremely competitive. Student groups compete for limited funds and are very aware of the organizations that receive funding. During the allocation process, one of the ethnic organizations presents a very detailed and compelling budget with many worthwhile programs outlined. It also presents a substantial fund-raising plan along with a marketing strategy for increasing its membership. As a result, the funding committee awards the organization approximately 50 percent of its requested budget. The average student organization receives 10 percent of its requested budget. One of the items that the committee decides to fund is promotional materials; it awards the organization $500. The organization will use these funds to purchase beach balls to give out as favors during the student organization recruitment fair. These items are promotional propaganda for the organization. Other student organizations are upset about the allocation, because they received only $500 in total funding and believe that funding should not be awarded for something as trivial as beach balls.

- What are the issues in this case?
- What are the committee's options for handling the situation? How might each one play out? Which option do you prefer?
- Regardless of whether you agree with the funding of beach balls, and considering that the committee has already made its decision, what would happen if the committee backed down and changed the allocation? What would be the consequences if the committee defended its allocation? What could be done if funding the beach balls was an oversight or an error made by the allocation committee? What might be the consequences if the committee decided to alter the allocation and then reversed its decision? Do you think that if the committee changed one allocation other organizations would want theirs changed as well?
- Have you ever had your allocations questioned? How did you handle the scrutiny? Did you change your allocation process as a result? Why or why not?

## Hiding Funds

The student activity fee application for funding requires that student organizations disclose any savings held by the organization as well as any fund-raising that they plan to do for the organization. Organizations soon learn not to fully disclose their savings to the allocation board, because those who have disclosed this information in the past have received less funding. The allocation committee justifies less funding by referring to the organization's savings as a source to fund the program. This frustrates many organizations because they view their savings as emergency funds. They believe that the allocation board is hypocritical when it comes to savings, because the board is required to save and spend wisely. Most organizations believe that the current system rewards organizations that spend their money frivolously and penalizes those that are fiscally responsible. Organizations want to know why they are being penalized for having rainy-day funds.

- What are the issues in this case?
- If you are a member of the allocation committee, what are your options for handling the situation? How might each option play out? Which option do you prefer?
- How do you handle organizations with savings? Do you allocate funds differently for those organizations that have substantial savings? Do you reward more money to organizations that do not have savings?
- How do you view fund-raising in your allocation process? Do you expect organizations to raise funds? If so, how much does their fund-raising ability weigh into your allocation process?

## Inside Advocate

The allocation of student organization funding is very political on your campus. Student organizations will do almost anything to get the "inside" edge on funding. One large and highly visible organization even goes so far as to "work the system" so that a member of the organization, whether appointed or elected, is always on the allocation committee. One of the policies of the allocation committee is that members cannot vote on or have a say in their student organization's allocations. Despite this rule, many "back door" deals in which one committee member vows to advocate for another committee member if that member supports the former's request are made. This strategy usually results in higher levels of funding for the advocate's organization, because the members of the committee are more informed about the program because someone is influencing the decision.

- What are the issues in this case?
- What are the allocation committee's options for handling the situation? How might each option play out? Which option do you prefer?
- Are members of your allocation committee involved in student organizations? Do you encourage their involvement? How do you know whether or not your committee members have similar agendas? How do you prevent bias from influencing your allocation decisions?
- Is politics part of the allocation process? Part of human nature? Is there any way to avoid politics as they relate to the allocation process? Should politics be avoided or encouraged? Should we teach college students how to "play the politics game" before they encounter it in the real world?
- If someone from one of the organizations seeking funding talked with allocation committee members in advance to explain his or her program, would that be acceptable? If someone asked the members to help advance his or her cause, would that be acceptable? Where do you draw the line between what is acceptable and not acceptable?

## Who Pays?

Sanborn University has undergone major budget cuts during the past two academic years. The division of student affairs in particular had to cut its budget by more than 30 percent over the past two years. This year it has been asked to cut another 10 percent. The vice president of student affairs informs you, the student government president and chair of the fee allocation committee, that she will need to cut the coordinator of student activities position. Lee, the full-time administrator who currently holds this position, coordinates most of the major events for the campus, including little siblings weekend, homecoming, and spring fling. She also advises the programming board and the student activity fee allocation committee. In addition, she registers all student organizations and processes all the paperwork associated with the student activity fee. Without a full-time person in this position, the university would have to consider canceling most of the major events and scale back on the other responsibilities that Lee currently covers.

The vice president asks you to consider using the carryover funds from the student activity fee to pay Lee's salary. Last year about $90,000 of the allocated $900,000 was not spent by the student organizations. When the student organizations fail to use their money by the end of the year, they lose it and the money is carried over to the next year for reallocation. Lee's salary and benefits would require about $45,000 annually. The vice president justifies using the carryover funds by reminding you of how much Lee supports the activity fee through overseeing the allocation process and day-to-day maintenance. It makes sense that her salary come from that pool of money, because she works directly with about $600,000 of the $900,000 budget. The vice president asks you to take the idea to the student government and the allocation committee for a vote. When you do so, some students feel pressured to support the initiative and argue that they shouldn't use the students' money to fund an administrative position. Others argue that if the fee didn't exist, the university wouldn't need Lee's position. In support of paying her salary, they argue that administering the fee is her job and that it should be paid for by the fund. You fear that if you cannot get the group to support the vice president's request she will ultimately decide to fund the coordinator position out of the student activity fee budget.

- What are the issues in this case?
- What are your options for handling the situation? How might each option play out? Which option do you prefer?
- How essential is it that someone serve in the coordinator role as described here? Does the support that that person gives to student organizations and to the university in general warrant financial support from the students?
- How do you feel about using the money to fund an administrative position? If your opinion differs from that of the vice president or the rest of the group, how heavily should your opinion weigh in? How much should you influence the decision?
- How do you feel knowing that the vice president might have already made her decision? How does that influence your decision? Have you ever been asked for your input but really felt that the decision had already been made? If so, how did you handle the situation?

## Embezzlement

Hector, a member of one of the funded student organizations, comes to you, the chair of the student allocation committee, with some concerns regarding

Louis, the president of his organization. Hector tells you that he is starting to question whether or not Louis is using the organization's money appropriately. Louis is the only person in control of the budget. He recently told the group that he needed a tape recorder, new office furniture, and a TV with a DVD player for the office. The group went along with his request because the items were for the whole organization, but slowly the items have been disappearing. One member thought he saw the TV and DVD player in Louis's apartment. Hector also tells you about a free conference that the group attended. Hector thinks that Louis might have made fake invoices (the funding board didn't know it was free) stating that there was a $100 registration fee and then pocketed the money. Finally, Hector tells you about a charity event that his organization held to raise money for a local children's shelter. The members sold tickets and also took donations at the door. Louis told the members that they made $300 on the event but Hector knows that they must have made at least $2,000. When Hector and the other members of the organization confronted Louis, he became very offensive and hostile and even threatened them. Student organization members are now fearful for their own safety.

- What are the issues in this case?
- What are your options for handling the situation? How might each option play out? Which option do you prefer?
- How should you go about investigating the accusations? When should you get your advisor and other university officials involved? When should you get the police involved?
- Have you ever had cases of embezzlement on your campus? If so, how were those instances handled? How difficult would it be for someone to embezzle funds from one of your student organizations? Are your policies and procedures clear about appropriate spending and misuse of funds?

## Signed Contract

The African American Student Alliance submits a last-minute request for funding of an event that includes a well-known speaker followed by a reception. As the allocation committee investigates the request, it discovers that the organization has already booked the speaker and signed a contract. The speaker alone costs $8,000 and the total request is for $10,000. The request is submitted two weeks prior to the event, and the allocation committee has serious concerns about the amount of time available to properly market the event. Additionally, the organization did not complete its funding packet correctly. On the funding application, it notes that the event will be cosponsored with the Office of Diversity, but when the allocation committee asks the director about the cosponsorship, she says she knows nothing about the event. The allocation committee denies the funding requests and sends the group a generic "no" letter.

The members of the African American Student Alliance are outraged. They claim racial discrimination and ask the vice president of institutional diversity to advocate for their program. The vice president calls the committee's advisor, who promptly explains the situation and the committee's justification. Since the contract is already signed, the vice president asks that the committee reverse the decision and fund the program. She will work with the organization to ensure that proper procedures are followed in the future.

- What are the issues in this case?
- If you were the chair of the allocation committee, what would your options be for handling the situation? How might each option play out? Which option do you prefer?
- Should you make an example out of the group or should you help it out? How could you prevent this from happening again either with this organization or with other organizations?
- What role does race play in this case? How do you feel about the vice president's influence?

## Multiple Roles

Your student allocation manual strongly encourages collaborative programming and joint sponsorship among organizations. Over the course of the year, you receive multiple funding requests from Ali Khan, president of the Muslim Student Association. It turns out that Ali is also president of the Arab American Student Association and the Middle East Coalition group.

Whenever he submits a request, he includes information about how the event is cosponsored by all three organizations. When you investigate further, you find out that most of the members of any one of Ali's organizations are also members of the other two organizations.

- What are the issues in this case?
- What are your options as they relate to future funding requests? How might each option play out? Which option do you prefer?
- Do you believe the events are actually cosponsored by the three organizations given that the membership among the three is almost identical? If the missions of the three organizations were all unique, would you believe that the events are cosponsored? What additional information do you need before making allocation decisions? How might you consider addressing this issue in your policies and procedures manual?
- How heavily does your allocation committee weigh cosponsorship? Are you more likely to fund a program if there are multiple sponsors?

## CASES APPROPRIATE FOR STUDENT PROGRAMMING BOARDS

## Budget Discrepancies

Each year the Office of Programming and Activities at UMB Community College holds two events for the students. Because students primarily commute to campus, the events are major and the budgets are large. Tamisha is the student coordinator of the spring event and works closely with Addison, another student leader on campus. The two work with their advisors from the Office of Programming and Activities but are given a great deal of autonomy to plan and carry out the event.

The extremely successful fall event included a nationally known comedian. For the spring event, the planning team decided to go with a musical group. Tamisha is friends with a man from a highly reputable local band that travels around to campuses across the country. The members of the planning team check out the band's Website, and they all agree that the group is extremely talented and would be a great act for the spring event. The band is booked and a price is negotiated. Tamisha agrees to take the lead on working with the band, processing the paperwork for payment, and travel. Addison handles all local arrangements, staging, and acoustics. Tonya, director of the Office of Programming and Activities, is quite impressed with their teamwork. She monitors their progress and oversees the budget and payment to the talent.

The well-attended event is a huge success, and the band is amazing. Tamisha and Addison are praised for their successful management. The dean of students is so impressed that she takes them both out for lunch to congratulate them. UMB has worked very hard to engage students outside the classroom, so having two successful events in one year is a big deal.

During the final budget analysis, Tonya notices some expenses that did not go through her but were paid out to Tamisha and Addison. She finds the reimbursement forms and sees that her signature is on the forms, but she does not remember signing them. She looks up the dates on the forms and realizes she was on vacation during that week. She calls in her assistant, Betty, who processes all the paperwork, and asks her what she knows about the reimbursements. She says that she remembers Tamisha and Addison bringing in the forms and that they told her Tonya had signed them before leaving for vacation. Tonya knows that she did not sign any incomplete forms, because UMB is extremely strict about reimbursements and no form is to be signed without being fully completed. She could lose her job for signing an incomplete form and giving it to a student. Tonya hates to jump to conclusions but it looks like Tamisha and Addison made up some expenses for their own personal benefit.

- What are the issues in this case?
- What are Tonya's options for handling the situation? How might each option play out? Which option do you prefer?
- Should Tonya talk with Tamisha and Addison first or go to the dean?

## Board Members Misbehaving at an Event

Every year your programming board hosts a major concert. Most members of the organization are involved in the planning, ticket sales, promotion, setup, and teardown. Many of the general board members are assigned to security and crowd control at the concert. They are asked to be professional but also encouraged to enjoy themselves. Two of the female general board members who are supposed to help with crowd control are dancing provocatively during the concert and flirting with the tech staff. As the chair of the concert committee, you tell them to stop and pay attention to managing the crowd. They ignore your request and keep grinding and flirting.

- What are the issues in this case?
- What are your options for handling the situation? How might each option play out? Which option do you prefer?
- How do the general members' actions reflect back on the organization as a whole? How do you balance your role as an organizational member with being able to enjoy the concert? How would you define being "professional" at the concert? How would you define "enjoying" the concert?
- What changes would you implement at the next concert to prevent a similar situation?

## Comedian Walks Off Stage

Robert is the president of the student programming board at Robinson Community College. Planning well-attended programs and events at a community college is always a challenge. All the students commute to campus, so they are typically only on campus for their classes, which makes finding a good time to schedule an event where there will be a captive audience difficult. One prime programming time is the lunch hour, when many people are gathered at the cafeteria. Although most students ignore the booked talent, some do enjoy noontime bands, comedians, and performers.

Robert and the programming committee book a comedian for a lunch break. The comedian, not forewarned about the venue and the participants' lack of interest, begins his routine. The audience is unresponsive. Some people are talking on cell phones, others are studying, and others are engaged in small-group work. The comedian quickly becomes frustrated by the lack of response, and within ten minutes of starting his performance, he walks off stage.

- What are the issues in this case?
- What are the options for handling the situation? How might each option play out? Which option do you prefer?
- Should you continue to program in this venue? What should you tell performers in advance of their performance? What might you do to get better participation from the students?

## Diversify the Talent

As the chair of the Student Programming Board, each spring you ask the programming chairs to submit their list of performers for the following year. Your comedy chair, Cindy, presents you with a list of four performers; the comedians will provide two performances per semester. She informs you that she met with the members of her committee and that they reviewed many tapes and believe that they have given you four outstanding performers. When you review the list, you realize that all four performers are White males. You bring this to Cindy's attention but she stands by the committee's decision, stating that the campus is 94 percent White, which should mean that the comedians will appeal to the majority of students.

- What are the issues in this case?
- If you were the president of the programming board, what would your options be? How might each option play out? Which option do you prefer?
- What message would you send by overriding Cindy's decision? What message would you send by sponsoring four White male performers?
- How should you approach the situation with Cindy?

## Hit the Big Time

Each spring the programming board sponsors the annual spring concert, the biggest event of the year for your organization. For this daylong event, your group tries to book a series of bands that are somewhat known to your students but that have yet to "make it big."

In September you book a band for the spring series. The contract is signed. Your concert committee really likes the band's music and believes that the band will be well received by the students. Over the course of the fall and spring semesters, the band grows in popularity. It becomes well known nationally and has two major hits. Your concert committee is thrilled. A month before the spring concert, the band wins a Grammy. Two days later, you get a call from the band's agent. He cancels the gig because of the band's increased popularity. The band is now earning ten times the amount of your contract and is no longer willing to play your venue.

- What are the issues in this case?
- What are your options for handling the situation? How might each option play out? Which option do you prefer?
- How should you respond to the agent? Should your group be willing to pay the difference to host the band? How binding is the contract?
- Do you knowingly run the risk of something like this happening when you book "emerging" talent?

## Who Is Getting the Talent?

A major speaker/big-time celebrity is due to speak on your campus Thursday night. As the major events chair, you are responsible for planning and coordinating the event. The entertainer is due to arrive at the airport at the same time that you have class. You ask the members of your committee if someone can pick her up, but all decline because of class conflicts. You must decide whether you should skip class to pick up the speaker or find another alternative.

- What are the issues in this case?
- What are your options for handling the situation? How might each option play out? Which option do you prefer?
- If you are eager to meet the performer, what should you do?
- Should you pick up an artist by yourself? What are your policies for transporting artists? What are the potential risks if you go alone?
- How do you prioritize your responsibilities? Do your organizational commitments ever take precedence over your academic priorities? How do you find the right balance?

## Pot-Smoking Band

Dave and Joe agree to pick up tonight's band from the airport. On the way back to campus, the three band members start passing around a fifth of whiskey and then a joint. Dave asks them to put it out and they refuse.

- What are the issues in this case?
- What are Dave and Joe's options for handling the situation? How might each option play out? Which option do you prefer?
- What would be the consequences if the confrontation leads to the band refusing to play at the concert?
- When should the agent be informed of the band members' behavior?

## Flirty Performers

A band performs on your campus Saturday night. Before, during, and after the performance, the band members keep flirting with two attractive female members of the programming board. After the performance, the band members want to go out and party and invite the women to join them.

- What are the issues in this case?
- What are the options for handling the situation? How might each option play out? Which option do you prefer?
- If the women are attracted to the band members and think it would be cool to party with them, should they go along with them? What are the risks involved if they decide to consume alcohol with the performers?
- Does your organization have a policy about fraternizing with performers? What would be the consequences if you strictly prohibit fraternization with the talent and the executive board members still go out with the band? How do you address the situation if you are the president of the organization?

## Limiting Freedom of Speech

Your major speakers chair and her committee decide to bring a controversial antiabortion speaker to campus. Your campus is very conservative and most students are antiabortion. Members of the administration express their concern with the decision because of the ensuing protests, negative press, and overall uproar about this speaker's scheduled appearance. They ask you to have the speaker "tone down" her message for the appearance.

- What are the issues in this case?
- What are your options for handling the situation? How might each option play out? Which option do you prefer?
- If the dean of students asks you to cancel the event and you refuse, would you run the risk of the administration canceling the speaker's appearance? What factors do you need to consider prior to making your decision?
- Have you ever had administration step in and influence your programming decisions? Does it have the right to intervene? Does it matter if your school is a private or public one?

## Appropriate Act for Sibs Weekend

Your comedy chair and his committee book a comedian to perform during little siblings' weekend. The audience consists of college students and their siblings ranging in age from eight to eighteen. The comedian starts using vulgar language and makes jokes that contain sexual content. Although his contract clearly states that he is performing for sibs weekend, his performance is not appropriate for younger children. Five minutes into the event you know that you are in trouble and will get many calls from angry parents complaining about the inappropriateness of this comedian's performance.

- What are the issues in this case?
- What are your options for handling the situation? How might each option play out? Which option do you prefer?
- Should you stop the event or let it continue? What are the potential consequences of doing each?
- If the comedian was making fun of the university's president and the president was in the room and was obviously getting angry, should you stop the event?

- Have you ever had to stop an event? What would be the steps or procedures involved in stopping an event?
- How could you prevent something like this from happening in the future? Should you get the agent involved?

## Holding Friends Accountable

Often it is the case that among programming boards executive board members become good friends. Lamar signs up to help with the setup for a sponsored event and then doesn't show up. Evelyn ends up doing most of the setup herself. Lamar is one of her good friends, and when she sees him, he apologizes for missing the event. He claims that he was sick and that it won't happen again.

- What are the issues in this case?
- What are Evelyn's options for handling the situation? How might each option play out? Which option do you prefer?
- Should Evelyn believe Lamar's excuse and hope that it doesn't happen again? Should she confront him?
- Given that it is often typical at most events that not everyone shows up to complete his or her assigned task, how should you plan accordingly? What type of contingency plan should you come up with before an event?
- Is it harder to confront a friend? Why or why not? Do you expect more from your friends than you do other members of your organization?

## Interclub Dating

The president, Jonathan, and treasurer, Kimberly, of your organization have been on the programming board for the past two years. They have always been good friends, and in the past year they started dating. At first their dating was a little awkward for the executive board, but eventually everyone got used to the idea. About two weeks ago, Jonathan and Kimberly broke up. Their breakup has really affected the dynamics of the programming board. The women on the board are siding with Kimberly and the men are aligning with Jonathan. Meetings are very uncomfortable for everyone, and Jonathan and Kimberly won't even look at each other. They are obviously very hostile toward one another.

- What are the issues in this case?
- If you were the vice president, what would your options be for handling the situation? How might each option play out? Which option do you prefer?
- Is it the vice president's place to step in and say something or should you just hope the conflict passes?
- What is your organization's perspective on dating within the organization? What potential problems may arise from members dating one another?

## Advance Ticket Sales

You are so excited to have a major concert on your campus this year. The band is well known and very expensive. Everyone—students, faculty, staff, alumni, community members—wants a ticket. Half of the available tickets are for students and half are for the rest of the university community. Of course, everyone wants the best seats. The week before the tickets go on sale, you receive a call from the president's office requesting four advance tickets for the president and his family. As the concert chair, you are more than willing to agree to the request. The office pays for the tickets, so money isn't an issue. Throughout the week, though, you continue to receive calls from the president's secretary requesting more tickets for members of the board of trustees and major donors. Again, the president's office pays for all the tickets, but you are struggling with whether or not it should have access to the tickets before they go on sale to students. You also wonder if this is a violation of the contract spelling out the conditions for ticket sales.

- What are the issues in this case?
- What are your options for handling the situation? How might each option play out? Which option do you prefer?

- Do you sell advance tickets within your organization? How do you decide who should receive that privilege? Is it okay to sell advance tickets to "dignitaries"?
- In this case, the tickets were paid for, but what would be your reaction if they were complementary? Have you ever been asked to give out a certain number of complementary tickets? If so, how did you decide who would receive them?

## Anti-Greek Advisor

It is well known that Angela, the programming board advisor, dislikes one of the fraternities. Nevertheless, several of this fraternity's members are active leaders on the programming board. During officer elections for the board, Jim, who is also a member of the disliked fraternity, runs unopposed for one of the positions. To lighten up the perceived boring speeches, he decides to give a humorous speech saying things such as, "I want the position because I think it's cool" and "I'll be able to meet more girls." The group laughs because they know Jim and appreciate his sense of humor. Angela, however, is outraged by the response and publicly expresses her distaste for Jim and his entire fraternity in front of the group. You, as the outgoing president, are chairing the officer election process.

- What are the issues in this case?
- What are your options for handling the situation? How might each option play out? Which option do you prefer?
- What should you do if you like Jim and know that he will do a good job for the organization despite his "inappropriate" attempt at humor?
- If you are a member of Jim's fraternity, what should you do? Would your reaction to the situation be different?

## Graduate Already!

Most of the executive board members of your campus programming group have been on the board for the past three years. They are extremely committed to the organization and struggle to give up being leaders to give others the opportunity. After two of these members graduate, they decide to pursue their graduate studies at the same institution. This will allow them to continue to participate in the organization. They give themselves the title of "graduate advisors" and continue to try to direct your organization. The advisor is nonconfrontational and doesn't have a problem with their continued domination of the programming board, but the undergraduate members are frustrated and want them gone. You are the current president of the organization.

- What are the issues in this case?
- What are your options for handling the situation? How might each option play out? Which option do you prefer?
- Why do you think the graduate students are still so committed to the organization?

# 9

# HONORARY/ACADEMIC/
# PROFESSIONAL
# ASSOCIATION CASES

## Conversion Therapy

Richard is the chair of the Gay/Lesbian Alliance Group at Ridgemore College in the Midwest. He is a senior electrical engineering major who has been an active student leader since his freshman year. As part of Richard's role he is allowed to sit on the interviewing team for new faculty members for departments across campus.

The English department is hiring a new faculty member, and Richard is asked to be a student representative on the committee. All students at Ridgemore College must take four years of English, so the student representative is selected from outside the major to diversify the input. In addition, the department is in need of a male voice, because most of the faculty members are women. Richard is excited about the opportunity and immediately begins reviewing the vitas. The search committee narrowed down the pool of candidates to seven for phone and then on-campus interviews. Richard is immediately alarmed when he reads that Dr. Evan Fuhr is a candidate. Dr. Fuhr is known for his conversion therapy camps where he works to help confused young adults find their true identity and true potential. Richard has read that what Dr. Fuhr really tries to do is scare gay and lesbian people into saying that they are heterosexual. Richard even had a friend in high school whose parents sent him off to this camp when he told them he was gay.

When the interview committee meets for the first time, Richard arrives ready to discuss all the candidates, whom he has rank ordered. He is not sure of the protocol at this point but is excited to be part of the process. He is shocked to find that all the other faculty members and one administrator on the committee have chosen Dr. Fuhr as their top candidate. "He is a modern-day literary genius," says one faculty member. "Yes, he would bring much prestige and recognition to this department. He may actually put Ridgemore College English Department on the map. Maybe then we can petition for our long-sought-after master's degree," comments another faculty member. Richard then speaks up: "I realize I am only a student and not even an English major, but I have some serious reservations about Dr. Fuhr and his beliefs." He goes on to tell the committee about the conversion therapy and cites articles demonstrating Dr. Fuhr's role. "I think that if we choose to interview him we will be sending a message that this college and department endorse such hateful and erroneous beliefs about one's identity. I don't think he should be interviewed," he concludes. Dr. Roberts, the department chair, replies, "Well, we certainly would not want to send that message, but really what he does in his private time is his business. We cannot censor every faculty member or administrator who walks through the door at Ridgemore. His scholarship and teaching records are impeccable, and frankly I think he makes a great candidate." Dr. Sandy, a senior faculty member, adds, "I think I have to agree with Dr. Roberts. However I feel about gays we cannot scrutinize everyone's private life." Richard, feeling quite defeated, leaves the meeting utterly dismayed and ashamed of the whole process. He does not quite know what to do now.

- What are the issues in this case?
- What are Richard's options for handling the situation? How might each option play out? Which option do you prefer?
- Do you think Richard should resign from the committee? Why or why not? Do you think he should use his role as a student leader to rally supporters and try to take on the administration? Why or why not?

## Behavior at Tailgate Parties

Tailgating before football games at Hoffman University is a long-held tradition in which most student groups participate. Each group has a designated area to set up its tailgate party. Bob is the vice president of the Education Honorary Society and Trisha is the secretary. They have been dating for a long time and are known by most students on campus. Both are excellent students and leaders in many student organizations.

Hoffman has a strict policy about student leaders not drinking at tailgate parties. The administration has enforced the policy on many occasions and feels that anyone who is elected or selected as a student leader should be a role model for other students on campus.

Each year Hoffman hosts a day for prospective freshmen and families to attend a football game, hear an admissions talk, and tour the campus. The tour is conducted prior to the game, because most families leave following the game. Bob is asked by the director of admission if the Education Honorary Society would be willing to provide student leaders to assist with a group at the game. He agrees to ask two of the group's members for their help. Regina, one of the volunteers, asks Bob, "What do I need to do?" He responds, "Talk to the families and help show them around campus before the game. I do have one favor, though. Please don't come near the student group area on Saturday. We are planning something fun and I don't think new students should see what we are doing." Regina agrees but is puzzled by his request.

On Saturday the admissions counselor begins the campus tour. As the group walks toward the south side of the stadium, where the student groups tailgate, Regina suggests, "Let's go the other way around the stadium." The admissions counselor replies, "I have to pick up the will-call tickets and they are on this side." Regina can't think of another excuse to alter their path. As they approach the student group area, she notices that a large group of students is gathered around a pickup truck. As they get closer, she realizes that a wet T-shirt contest is being held and that some of the women participating aren't even wearing T-shirts. She then sees that Trisha is a contestant and that Bob is in a fake tuxedo serving as the emcee. She is shocked. Bob is falling-down drunk and Trisha is wearing a thin, white, sopping wet T-shirt. Regina nearly stumbles as she turns to walk away. Bob comes running up to her and says, "This is really no big deal. Can you just pretend that you didn't see anything?"

- What are the issues in this case?
- What are Regina's options for handling the situation? How might each option play out? Which option do you prefer?

- How do you think Regina should proceed? What do you think should happen to Bob and Trisha? Given that the admissions counselor will report the incident, should the group take action or let the university system handle the situation?
- How do you think Regina, the Education Honorary Society, and the university should resolve the situation?
- Have you ever had to confront fellow students about inappropriate behavior that was in violation of university or your organization's policies? If so, how did you handle the situation?

## Forging a Letter of Recommendation

You get a phone message from a woman who works at a consulting company who is interested in speaking to you regarding a reference for Darnell, your former roommate and your co-chair of the Future Farmers of America Student Group at Inside College. Darnell graduated last year and has been looking for a job for a year. You were not aware that he had used your name as a reference, but you don't mind.

You are happy to talk up your friend, so you call the woman back. She tells you that she read the letter you wrote and is interested in hearing more about the student group. Surprised to hear this, you say, "I am not sure what letter you are referring to." She says that Darnell included a letter from you with his application as well as letters from two other individuals who were board members while you and Darnell were co-chairs. You are totally confused and positive that you did not write a letter for Darnell. You ask if she can fax the letter and she agrees.

When you receive the faxed letter, you are alarmed. Not only did Darnell forge the letter and signature, but he also forged the letterhead of the organization. Concerned that Darnell forged the letters that the woman said came from the two board members as well, you contact the board members and learn that they never wrote the letters.

- What are the issues in this case?
- What are your options for handling the situation? How might each option play out? Which option do you prefer?

- Should your response relate in any way to the nature of your relationship with Darnell? If after you confront him he tells you that he wrote the letters to save time, how should you respond?

## Racial Comments During a Class Project

Philosophy classes at Major Community College have student leaders who facilitate a portion of the class. At the beginning of the year, a group of faculty members select the leaders from the top students from the previous year. Steve and Alanya are selected to lead Dr. Warden's class during the fall semester. The two are doing an excellent job assisting with group projects. During one class session, Steve and Alanya are helping the student groups and Dr. Warden decides to walk around and monitor. He observes the group Steve is working with and hears Steve say, "We'll just Jew him down. That price is way too much." The other students in the group gasp in response to his comment.

- What are the issues in this case?
- What are Dr. Warden's options for handling the situation? How might each option play out? Which option do you prefer?
- What should Dr. Warden say to the other students?
- If the roles were reversed and Dr. Warden made the comment and Steve overheard it, how should Steve respond? Is it worse if a student makes such a comment or a faculty member? Who is more difficult to confront? Why?

## Come to My Party

Jodi is the current secretary of the Alpha Business Honorary Fraternity. The four other executive board members are men, so she often feels that the organization's social programming is male oriented. It usually revolves around sports and games, which do not interest her or the other female members.

To get more of the women involved, Jodi decides to have a party at her off-campus house. She recently learned about a person who does sex toy parties for women, and everyone she talked with who had attended these parties seemed to have had a good time. Jodi invites only the female fraternity members to the party. She keeps the products that will be discussed and displayed a secret from the women but tells them they will have a good time.

Ten women attend the ladies' night out and are shocked by the products. The sexually based items are offensive to many. Janice, one of the younger members, comes over to Jodi and says, "I am disgusted and offended that you would hold such a party. I really looked up to you before this. I am leaving!" Jodi is shocked by her reaction but is not dissuaded from continuing with the party. Four other women react similarly and leave very quickly. All of the guests except Jodi's roommate and one other woman end up leaving early.

- What are the issues in this case?
- What are Jodi's options for handling the situation? How might each option play out? Which option do you prefer?
- Do you think Jodi used her leadership position inappropriately? If so, in what ways?
- How should the other leaders of Alpha handle this situation? Do you think it should become an issue for the fraternity?
- How should the organization deal with its gender conflicts? Is it okay to have female only and male only events?

## Academic Summer Camp

Jake is the undergraduate student director of a weeklong academic camp. He was promoted to this role this year after serving in a camp counseling role the previous two years. His job includes living in the residence hall with the campers, overseeing the nightly programming, and supervising the ten other undergraduate camp counselors. Three hundred high school students from all over the United States are enrolled in the camp. The students are high achievers academically and must undergo a rigorous application process in order to be admitted to the camp. The camp also offers scholarships to high-achieving, low-income students.

This year two students who are on full scholarship have come from across the country to attend. The students were responsible for their airfare and lodging the day before the camp began. In the weeks prior to the camp, Jake spoke with the mother of Martin, one of the scholarship recipients, and assured her that her son would have many opportunities to meet other students and get a good feel for campus living.

On Monday, Jake gets a call from a faculty facilitator who states that two students failed to attend the morning academic session. The faculty is given strict instructions to take attendance and report any absences immediately. Because all the students are underage, it is important that they be accounted for at all times. The two students who missed the morning session happen to be the two full-scholarship students, Martin and Loredo.

This situation presents an interesting dilemma for Jake, because under normal circumstances the students would be dismissed immediately and sent home, but in this situation, Jake is well aware that Martin's mother is a single parent with no extra income to get an emergency flight for her son. Jake and the full-time camp director call the students into Jake's office. Both students provide an elaborate story about getting lost and say that that's why they missed the morning session. Jake gives them a stern warning and tells them that one more absence will result in an early trip home.

On Wednesday, Jake gets a call from a different faculty member who says that two students came late to the morning session and never returned after a short break. Not surprisingly, the students are Martin and Loredo. Jake calls them into his office again and this time he gets Martin's mother on the phone. Jake tells her about the second incident and that he must send Martin home. Jake further tells her that he will need the flight information so that he can personally get Martin to the airport and make sure he is safely on the flight. Martin's mother says that she has no money to assist but that Jake can release him even though he is sixteen years old and that he can stay at a local hotel until their original flight leaves on Saturday morning. Jake is well aware that this is against all camp and university rules and is not sure what to do.

- What are the issues in this case?
- What are Jake's options for handling the situation? How might each option play out? Which option do you prefer?
- With whom should Jake consult?
- What legal ramifications could the school face by releasing the students?

## Personal Life versus Professional Conduct

Teva Community College has an active chapter of an honor society for community college students seeking transfer to elite four-year schools. Students must be nominated by faculty based on academics, character, and community service. Dr. Wills is thinking about nominating Hramiec, an excellent student who is majoring in physics and has a 3.9 grade point average (GPA). Hramiec is an active service provider to the college and is well respected by students, faculty, and administrators. The one problem that Dr. Wills has with Hramiec is that he recently saw him getting a lap dance at a strip club close to campus. Hramiec was with a group of other students and appeared to be extremely intoxicated.

- What are the issues in this case?
- What are Dr. Wills's options for handling the situation? How might each option play out? Which option do you prefer?
- Should Dr. Wills put his reputation on the line for Hramiec?
- Should what Hramiec does in his own time affect his academic reputation?
- How would you proceed if you were Dr. Wills?

## Pub Crawl

Jason is the president of the Student Business Council (SBC) at a major research university. The SBC has one representative from each of the academic organizations affiliated with the College of Business. As president, Jason is responsible for conducting the meetings, making sure all funds are dispersed to each group, and bringing the organizations together during National Business Week. The week is a way to promote business majors; bring college faculty, staff, and students together for some friendly competition; and raise money for a preselected charity. Events include a dunk tank, a date auction, a mock rock evening, an academic decathlon, and a major showcase event. The week runs from Monday to Thursday evening, and by the end of the week everyone is tired and ready to unwind.

Jason decides that it would be fun to set up a pub crawl for Thursday night, have T-shirts made with all the bar names on it, and add a little competition. The majors within business that have the most participants will win. When Jason discusses the event with Kia, the vice president, she asks him, "How do you plan to advertise?" He responds, "I have access to the collegewide listserv and I will just post a message about the final event on that." She then asks, "Do you think that is a good idea since this isn't an official event affiliated with National Business Week and it is promoting the use of alcohol?" He replies, "I can't imagine why that would be a problem. I've been out to the bar with some professors before, and I'm sure they won't care. I bet they'll join us."

On Wednesday afternoon, Jason sends out the message to the e-mail list and heads off to class. About an hour later, the dean of the college storms out of her office and heads to the student affairs office, where the SBC offices are housed.

- What are the issues in this case?
- What are the dean's options for handling the situation? How might each option play out? Which option do you prefer?
- What do you think the dean should do? Should Jason be punished?
- How should the college handle this situation and what can it do to prevent future situations like this?

## Who Are You?

Lola is the undergraduate student representative of the board of trustees at DNT College, a small liberal arts college. Student leaders in general are well respected by faculty, administrators, and students. The student representative appointment to the board of trustees is competitive and students campaign to get elected.

Lola is a below average engineering student who was denied admission to the engineering program. Her GPA is well below the minimum required for admission, and she has been strongly advised to look at alternate majors or transfer to another school with a less competitive program. Lola is a very involved leader at DNT and transferring to another school and applying to its engineering program is not really an option. She changes her major but intends to reapply for engineering when she gets her grades up after repeating a class this semester.

Despite her below average grades, Lola is an excellent leader and well respected around campus. Halfway through the semester, she is asked to talk to a group of incoming freshmen about life at DNT and ways to get involved. The associate director of admissions asks her to tell him a little bit about herself so he'll be prepared when he introduces her to the group of freshmen. She tells him about her involvement with various groups and her dreams following graduation. He asks what her major is and she tells him that it is engineering.

- What are the issues in this case?
- What are the options for handling the situation? How might each option play out? Which option do you prefer?

# Honorary Induction

You are president of your academic honorary. M.J. is the vice president of the organization and is responsible for coordinating the annual induction ceremony for new members. About a week before the scheduled induction, M.J. informs you that she is too busy to coordinate the event. You learn that she really hasn't started planning the event. The room isn't reserved, the refreshments haven't been ordered, and the props are still in storage. Although you scold her for dropping the ball, you know that the job still needs to get done.

- What are the issues in this case?
- What are your options for handling the situation? How might each option play out? Which option do you prefer?
- Are you the type of leader who would step in and organize the event? Have you ever had to set up and get the job done in the past? Why did you decide on this course of action? Were there others you could rely on or was the event at a critical point when you needed to ensure that things were done and done correctly?

# Relationship with the Department Secretary

As the president of your academic honorary association, you work closely with the department's secretary, Darlene. Darlene continually scolds you for doing too much and for neglecting your studies. At the same time, she knows that you are the type of person who cannot say no when asked to do something. She often asks you to participate in faculty search committees, admissions tours, and planning events for the department. You know that Darlene asks you because you are a dedicated student leader who is good with follow-through. You are also flattered and grateful that she seeks your assistance. Although you appreciate the recognition and opportunity to be involved, you are also starting to feel overwhelmed.

- What are the issues in this case?
- What are your options for handling the situation? How might each option play out? Which option do you prefer?
- Have you ever felt conflicted between wanting to be involved and knowing that if you are you will feel overwhelmed because you are doing too much? How do you find the appropriate balance?
- How hard is it for you to say no? What will happen if you say no?
- When prioritizing the items on your plate, how do you decide which ones to let go?

# Please Be Our Treasurer

Tanner has been in your organization for only a semester. The previous treasurer left school, and the organization desperately needs a replacement, so the president asks Tanner to take over the position. Tanner quickly discovers that the financial records are in disarray. He believes the former treasurer was very inexperienced and held the position only in title. There is no record of expenditures, and this leaves Tanner with no sense of the organization's monetary situation. He decides to go to the bank and sit down with one of the tellers to get the details of the account. It takes four hours for the bank employee and Tanner to balance the organization's checkbook.

Tanner calls a meeting for the following day to update the members on their finances. He informs them that even though it is only halfway into the school year the organization has spent almost its entire budget. Only about one tenth of the budget remains. The members of the group don't believe what Tanner tells them about the state of their finances. They want to continue to spend liberally and are opposed to the limits that Tanner wants to place on spending. Tanner has also set up the checking account so that two signatures are required on every check, and this too upsets the members.

- What are the issues in this case?
- What are Tanner's options for handling the situation? How might each option play out? Which option do you prefer?
- Should Tanner have approached the situation differently?
- Should the organization's members be resistant to change? Why or why not?
- How do you control spending in your organization? How closely is spending monitored beyond the treasurer? Does your organization have a budget?

# SERVICE LEARNING ORGANIZATIONS/COMMUNITY ENGAGEMENT CASES

## Unresponsive Leadership in AmeriCorps

### by Natalie Jackson

S tan, the leader of an AmeriCorps team, recently received the following letter from his disgruntled team. Prior to receipt of the letter, Stan thought the team was productive and working well together. Although he was a new team leader, he thought the team respected him for his dedication to the program and focus on team unity.

Dear Team Leader,

We are writing this letter because you have been unreceptive to our previous expressions of concern about our AmeriCorps team and your leadership. It is our hope that this letter will help to facilitate the communication that has been lacking between the team corps members and yourself.

The ten of us came to the AmeriCorps base camp three months ago from around the country. As recent college graduates passionate about public service, we were energized and eager to meet our teammates and team leader and to head off to our first service project. Although our orientation and in-processing seemed very disorganized and irrelevant, our enthusiasm was still uncurbed. However, once assigned to the desert trenching project in Arizona, many of us experienced disturbing interactions with you even in your first week as team leader. Our frustration has only continued to grow as a result of these conflicts.

The arbitrary and impractical rules that you have imposed on us have made us question whether you have our best interests and well-being in mind as our team leader. Why, in the 100-plus-degree heat of the desert, are we not permitted to roll up our uniform sleeves while we are doing demanding physical work? Although the sleeve issue may seem like a small point of contention, this complaint is just one example of the inappropriate ways in which you exercise your authority over the team members. Instead of supporting your team members and working to build team skills, it seems that you resent us and view team unity as a threat to your authority.

Again we questioned your view of "teamwork" in Utah at the food bank assignment. The turmoil created between yourself and the food bank supervisor as the two of you fought over who was "in charge" of us led to much discomfort and confusion in the work environment. We were there to fulfill our assignment—to provide food for hungry and homeless people—but this somehow got lost as the power struggle continued. Our mission has been completely clouded by your treatment of us.

Throughout these three months, we have felt your attempts to divide our team, whether by gender, skill level, or in some other way. You seem uncomfortable with a unified team and intimidated by anyone who exhibits strength. The misery that such leadership has caused each of us is indescribable. Our spirit and energy are drained with each passing day. Each and every one of us is questioning whether we can fulfill our year obligation under these conditions. We do not want to be quitters—but none of this seems worth it. We are all at a breaking point. If we cannot work together to make some changes, our AmeriCorps team will fall apart. It is our hope that you believe our mission and team are worth saving and that you will communicate with us on these issues.

Sincerely,
Team Corps Members

- What are the issues in this case from the perspective of the team members as well as of the AmeriCorps team leader?
- If you were the AmeriCorps team leader, what would your options be for handling the situation? How might each option play out? Which option do you prefer?
- If you were the team leader, what could you have done earlier on to solicit feedback from the team members?
- Have you ever worked on a team where you felt the leader did not have the best interests of the team at heart? If so, how did you approach the situation?

# Medical Emergency

Brenda has been participating in the summer camp program at her college for three years and loves every minute of it. She worked her way up from a camp counselor to a group leader and now supervises all the counselors on her site and is responsible for their training. She is an elementary education major and feels that this experience not only has verified her choice of major but will make her a better teacher in the future. Brenda is also highly regarded by her peers and the full-time camp staff. Time and time again she has assumed leadership positions. Her staff loves her and looks to her for guidance and direction on a daily basis.

During her senior year, Brenda is serving as a group leader for a summer camp program for low-income high school students when she notices a large red spot on her right thigh. Since she has an appointment for a routine checkup with her doctor the next week, she decides to wait until then to have the spot examined. When Brenda visits the doctor, she mentions the spot and says that it is probably not a big deal. He examines the spot and says that she should schedule a biopsy immediately, because it looks suspicious. A week later she has the biopsy and finds out that she has advanced basal cell melanoma. The doctor advises her to have surgery immediately, to prevent the spread of the disease. Brenda is devastated and immediately calls her parents for advice. They tell her that she should come home and that they will have their family friend who is a dermatologist and specializes in basal cell melanoma perform the surgery. Brenda is not sure that this is what she really needs to do; after all, there are only five weeks left in the summer, and her staff and campers really need her. Brenda wonders, "What will they do without me? Who will step into my role?" Brenda has many questions.

- What are the issues in this case?
- What are Brenda's options for handling the situation? How might each option play out? Which option do you prefer?
- Do you think Brenda's feelings that she will be abandoning her staff and campers are accurate? Do you think Brenda is using her leadership role to fill another void in her life?
- What should Brenda and the camp staff do? What should Brenda do if she stays? What should she do if she departs early?

# Inappropriate Comments

Tina and Donna are roommates at a summer program that provides enrichment opportunities to elementary-age students across the country. They have been working with the program since they were freshmen and now they are in the summer preceding their senior year. The program operates at locations all over the United States as well as around the world. This summer the two are working in a low-income neighborhood outside Los Angeles, California. Both are excited because they are from small towns and they want to experience life in a larger city.

The program is going well. The kids appear to be enjoying the programs each day, and the staff gets along nicely. During the third week of the program, the weather is particularly rainy and uncooperative for outside programs. Many of the days are spent with everyone cramped inside working on art projects and other activities. At the end of the week, Tina and Donna decide that the staff needs to go out for a night on the town to blow off some steam. Most of the staff members agree and plan for a night in the city.

The group decides on an area that has many restaurants and bars so that they can take two cars and still have some options. At about 11:30 P.M., Tina asks Donna to come to the bathroom with her. In the ladies' room Tina tells Donna that Eric, a counselor from Boston, came up to her on the dance floor and started acting inappropriately. Tina says, "First, he started grinding at my leg, and then he said, 'Oh, baby, I could do this all night, but it would be more fun with no clothes on.'" Donna responds, "What did you say?" Tina replies, "I was a bit embarrassed and said I wasn't really interested, and I walked away." Donna then asks, "Did he follow you?" Tina answers, "No, but he did yell, 'What is up with you? Are you a lesbo or something?'" Shocked, Donna says, "He said that? I think you should report him to Maria, the camp director." Unsure of what to do, Tina replies, "I don't know—I've been drinking. Maybe it was my imagination."

- What are the issues in this case?
- What are Tina's options for handling the situation? How might each option play out? Which option do you prefer?
- If Tina reports the incident to Maria, what do you think they should do?

## We Don't Need Your Help

You are the president of a community outreach organization for Amble University, a private university located in an urban, low-income, predominantly Mexican community. The students are predominantly White and from upper- to middle-class families. As part of the service mission, your organization established a mentoring program in one of the local elementary schools. Students from Amble volunteer in the school for one or two hours per week. It quickly becomes apparent that many of the students are failing to connect with the children. They struggle to understand why the parents are not teaching their children English, why education is not more of a priority for the students, and how they can live in poverty. The teachers are starting to complain about the students' inability to understand the needs of the children.

- What are the issues in this case?
- What are your options for handling the situation? How might each option play out? Which option do you prefer?
- Is it possible that some of the misunderstanding comes from the students' inabilities to relate to students of a different ethnicity and socioeconomic status? What could you do to better prepare the students to participate in the program?

## Political Support

Julia is an officer of the Young Democrats, an active political organization. This year is a presidential election year and the members of the organization favor one candidate. They cannot use student organization–allocated funds to support an individual candidate, so Paul, one of the organization's members, suggests that they create a new organization with the same members of the Young Democrats. The new organization can receive funding to promote voter registration and encourage people to vote. During the voting drives and registration events, Julia and the others can post candidate signs and even mention to those signing up that they should consider their candidate. This way the organization can use monies they earned from fund-raising to support the favored candidate.

- What are the issues in this case?
- What are the options for handling the situation? How might each option play out? Which option do you prefer?
- What do you think of Paul's strategy? Is it ethical?

## Too Much Delegation

Every year your organization coordinates a zoo trip for a group of local disadvantaged youth. Cameron is the president of the organization and he tends to delegate everything. Most of the members wonder what he actually does as president. David is the vice president and often the person who receives most of the delegated tasks. David has difficulty saying no and is getting overwhelmed and frustrated because Cameron keeps dumping things on him. Cameron asks David to coordinate the zoo field trip. David gets upset by the request and is ready to quit the organization.

- What are the issues in this case?
- What are David's options for handling the situation? How might each option play out? Which option do you prefer?
- Why is it easier for David to consider quitting the organization than to confront Cameron? Have you ever been tempted to just walk away from a conflict rather than deal with it? If so, why?
- What do you think David should say to Cameron?

## Holding Friends Accountable

Carol is the president of her service organization and her roommate, Melinda, is the vice president. Although their living situation is really good and they are great friends, Melinda isn't a very good vice president. She lacks follow-through, gossips during meetings, and doesn't provide much leadership for the organization. Carol decides to subtly reassign most of Melinda's vice presidential responsibilities rather than hold her accountable, because

Carol doesn't wish to mess up their living situation and Melinda's friendship means more to her than does Melinda's ability to plan a program.

- What are the issues in this case?
- What are the options for handling the situation? How might each option play out? Which option do you prefer?
- What is your opinion of Carol's decision? Would you handle the situation the same way? Why or why not?
- If Melinda is not held accountable, can Carol hold other members of the organization accountable? Why or why not?
- If Carol confronts Melinda, what should she say to her?

## Getting Younger Members Involved

Your organization has only ten members. Three of the members are seniors, and they have been members since they were freshmen. Because the three seniors know everything about the organization, they tend to run all the meetings, organize all the events, apply for campus programming funds, and coordinate all aspects of the organization. They don't delegate responsibility or make an effort to include new members. Underclassmen attend meetings but eventually stop coming because they don't feel involved.

- What are the issues in this case?
- What are your options for handling the situation? How might each option play out? Which option do you prefer?
- Why are the seniors so committed to their organization? Do you think their actions are justified?
- Why is it important for the seniors to include new members? If they fail to delegate to new members and bring them into the organization, what is the likelihood of the organization surviving?
- Who should bring the current problem to the attention of the seniors, and how?
- Have you ever been part of an organization where you felt that only a few members ran the organization? How did you handle the situation?

# Skimming

Elaine, the president of the Alternative Breaks organization, is found guilty of embezzling money from another student organization. According to the incident report, she embezzled $500 by writing checks to cash from the organization's account. Alternative Breaks has had no trouble with Elaine. She's been a strong leader and has coordinated most of the details for the upcoming spring break trip to Belize. A record number of students are signed up for the trip, and Elaine should be credited for the increased participation, because she's worked really hard on organizing this trip. As vice president of the Alternative Breaks organization, you now need to decide if, given the allegations, Elaine should be allowed to go on the trip.

- What are the issues in this case?
- What are your options for handling the situation? How might each option play out? Which option do you prefer?
- Whom should you consult before making the decision? What should you do if your organization's bylaws don't provide any direction?

# Habitat

Every year the campus organization of Habitat for Humanity builds a house for a needy family. In the past two years, however, the organization has selected families who didn't meet the obligations of the Habitat contract. In one case, despite multiple warnings, the family didn't complete their service hours to help build their home. In the other case, one of the parents was arrested for armed robbery when the house was still being built. In both cases, eventually the organization advisor had to tell the families that they would not receive the house. These two negative experiences really took their toll on the morale of the group. This year there are even fewer applicants, and the group is determined to select a worthwhile family who will fulfill the obligations outlined in the contract. They do not have a stellar applicant, so the group debates whether to take a risk on a less qualified family or start building the house and hope that they will eventually find a family who will meet the criteria. They feel trapped. They don't want another bad experience but have also learned that building a house for no one equals less commitment from the group.

- What are the issues in this case?
- What are the group's options for handling the situation? How might each option play out? Which option do you prefer?
- Is motivation ever a problem for your organization? If so, how do you hold members accountable and still keep them motivated to participate?

## Conflicts with a Larger Affiliation

For financial reasons, your college chapter of Habitat for Humanity is affiliated with a local community chapter. Although the two groups have separate building projects, separate constitutions, and separate memberships, the community chapter keeps trying to impose its views on the student organization. The members of the community chapter want to be involved in every step of the process, including selecting the family, choosing the design of the house, reviewing the financial information, and establishing a time line. Although some of their help is appreciated, the college chapter is getting very frustrated with their over-involvement. The membership of your organization asks Jackson, the president, to confront members of the community chapter and demand that they become less involved.

- What are the issues in this case?
- What are Jackson's options for handling the situation? How might each option play out? Which option do you prefer?
- If the student organization is financially dependent on the community organization, does the community organization then have more of a say in the day-to-day operations?
- How do you achieve a reasonable balance between receiving valuable advice from the community chapter and having everything your organization does scrutinized by them?

# Timing Your Publicity

Your community outreach organization coordinates an annual Halloween party for children in the community. You select a date, plan the event, and market it to the community. Although fifty kids sign up, only five attend the event. When you evaluate why the attendance was so low, you receive feedback that the promotional materials went out too early (three weeks before the event), and people forgot about the party. Since the party was free, although people signed up, their level of commitment was low.

- What are the issues in this case?
- What are some things that the organization could do to prevent something like this from happening again? Would sending reminder e-mails or collecting money for the event when people sign up be helpful?
- How much lead time works for your organization when planning events? How far in advance should the promotional materials be distributed? Do you remind people of an event as the date for it approaches? When purchasing food or other materials for an event, do you estimate attendance? If so, how do you do so?

# Healthy Choices

One of the missions of your organization is to facilitate a mentoring program between college students and elementary students in the community. College mentors are required to do something with their students at least once a month. This month your organization decides to host an arts and crafts day for mentors and their protegés. This is a great opportunity for the pairs to spend time together. In addition to coordinating the arts and crafts, your organization provides lunch for the children. Some of the parents complain to your advisor because the lunch choices of pizza, cookies, and punch are not healthy. Upon hearing the criticisms, many members of the organization become very upset. They have just planned a wonderful, *free* event for children in the community, and all the parents can do is complain. Many members are ready to quit. They feel that their time and energy go unappreciated.

- What are the issues in this case?
- If you were one of the organizational leaders, what would your options be for handling the situation? How might each option play out? Which option do you prefer?
- Are the parents' concerns justified? Why or why not?
- Are the students' negative responses to the parents justified? Why or why not?
- How would you convince the members to stay committed to the mentoring program?

# Ineffective Advisor

Your organization needs to request student activity fee funding to put on an event for the campus. Your proposed event is a speaker followed by small-group discussion. The request is due next week and you need your advisor to sign off on the proposal. You give her the proposal in a timely manner, but more than a week after she receives the proposal, she still hasn't returned it with her signature. Your advisor really is not actively involved in your organization. Her delay is just another sign of her lack of involvement.

- What are the issues in this case?
- What are your options for handling the situation? How might each option play out? Which option do you prefer?
- What is the role of your organization's advisor? How is that role communicated? Does your advisor have a clear understanding of his or her role and the expectations of the organization? Are those expectations realistic?
- Have you talked with your advisor about how much time he or she has to dedicate to your organization?

# Retention of Members

The World Peace Initiative organization has retention problems. The organization typically has sixteen people for the first meeting of the year, then ten, then eight, then six, and then two or three. Marisol is the organization's president, and she is extremely dedicated to the organization. She works tirelessly for peace initiatives. She coordinates demonstrations and has marched several times in Washington, D.C. Although her passion is commendable, obviously, not every member of the organization is as into activism as Marisol. Some join the organization because they want to discuss peace initiatives and debate the war. When it comes to protests and activism, however, they are not as confident as Marisol.

At a recent meeting of the remaining three members, Marisol recommends that the organization consider additional incentives to attract people to the meetings. She suggests providing pizza at the meetings. Oliver, the vice president, wants to recommend that the organization change its mission and make involvement a more reasonable time commitment, but he is scared to speak up.

- What are the issues in this case?
- What are Oliver's options for handling the situation? How might each option play out? Which option do you prefer?
- Why do you think Oliver is hesitant to speak up? Should he confront Marisol? If so, what should he say to her? Can the organization serve the needs of multiple constituents? If so, how?
- Have you ever asked the members of your organization what they want out of the organization and how much time they have to contribute to it? Why or why not? Is it right to assume that all members of an organization are as dedicated as its leadership?

## Where Are the Volunteers?

Every year your organization coordinates an event entitled "Be My Neighbor Day." This event takes place on a Saturday. Students are put into groups of ten and assigned a project within the community. Some groups paint houses, others fix roofs, and some clean up local parks. The community really appreciates the work that the students do. This year 150 people sign up to participate in this community service volunteer day. However, when the volunteer day arrives, about 75 people show up, but the coordinator has projects allocated for all 150.

- What are the issues in this case?
- What are the coordinator's options for handling the situation? How might each option play out? Which option do you prefer?
- How might the coordinator have prevented such a low turnout?
- Since the community is relying on the coordinator and the organization to complete the assigned tasks, what should the coordinator do and how should it be communicated?

## Grandparents' Project

One of the major initiatives of your service organization is the adopt-a-grandparent program. Your organization coordinates regular visits by the students to a local nursing home. The activities director of the nursing home event invited you to hold your organization's meetings there. Cody, the president of the organization, calls the activities director a week before the first meeting to remind her that twenty-five people are planning to come to the nursing home. A week later, the members arrive at the home with food and events planned for the seniors only to find that the activities director forgot about the meeting. Cody is very frustrated, because before beginning the program, the activities director made a huge deal about the students keeping their promises to the seniors by showing up for their regularly scheduled visits, but the director obviously doesn't practice what she preaches. She wants the grandparents' program to be a priority for the students but doesn't make it a priority for herself. The director suggests that the group come back another day. Cody and the students go home discouraged and angry.

- What are the issues in this case?
- What are Cody's options for handling the situation? How might each option play out? Which option do you prefer?
- Should Cody talk with the director? If so, what should he say to her?
- How should Cody encourage the students to maintain their commitment to the adopt-a-grandparent program?

## Failure to Communicate

Faith and Joy are working with a community agency to plan a track and field day for children. Faith, Joy, and the members of their organization are coordinating the college student volunteers, the games, and the prizes. The community agency is in charge of promotion, snacks, and registration. The event planners expect to draw about 100 elementary school children. Three days before the event, the community agency cancels the event and fails to contact either Faith or Joy. The agency reschedules for another day without consulting them. Faith and Joy learn about the cancellation from the person in charge of reserving the event space on campus, who informs them that the date was changed because not enough children wanted to participate on the date selected.

- What are the issues in this case?
- What are Faith and Joy's options for handling the situation? How might each option play out? Which option do you prefer?
- Do you think Faith and Joy should confront the community agency representative? What should they do if they want to maintain a good working relationship with the agency?
- Have you ever worked collaboratively with a community agency or another group? If so, did you establish clear expectations for each group when planning the event? Why or why not? Would you recommend this strategy for Faith and Joy?

## Earth Day Celebration

As part of the annual Earth Day celebration, Hillary's organization wants to coordinate a campus clean-up project. Students would volunteer to pick up trash, sweep sidewalks, weed flower beds, and do whatever else is necessary to beautify the campus. Hillary's organization is very excited about this opportunity. The dean of students recommends that she contact the facilities department before she starts planning the cleanup, because it may be an issue with the facilities union. In contacting Rupert, the director of facilities, Hillary learns that the cleanup would indeed be an issue with the union. Despite the request to cancel the event, Hillary still wants to proceed. She advocates for the clean-up day with the dean of students and with the vice president of business operations, but they still won't let Hillary's group facilitate the event. Hillary and her group are very frustrated.

- What are the issues in this case?
- What are Hillary's options for handling the situation? How might each option play out? Which option do you prefer?
- Should Hillary's group defy administration and still proceed with the clean-up day? Should they coordinate the clean-up day in the community rather than on campus? Should they not have the clean-up day?
- Have you ever been excited about an idea for a program and had administration disagree with it or demand that you not facilitate the program? If so, did you do what you wanted to do or did you do what the administration wanted you to do? Why?

## Advisor Who Does It All

Judy, the advisor of your organization, is also a full-time employee of the university. Although you appreciate her initiative and support of your organization, sometimes she does things without informing the group. For example, when Ian was coordinating a fundraiser for the organization, Judy called him to see if he had ordered the giveaways for the event. The very same day, you, the president of the organization, called him to ask the same question. Once you talked with Ian you learned that Judy had already called. In addition, sometimes Judy reserves rooms for your weekly meetings and makes drafts of the budget. Again, you appreciate her help, because a lot of advisors are in "name only," but sometimes you think she does too much.

- What are the issues in this case?
- What are your options for handling the situation? How might each option play out? Which option do you prefer?
- How should you approach Judy with your concerns? What should you say to her?
- Should you and Judy establish expectations for each other? If so, how should you decide the expectations? Should you also establish a time

frame to revisit the expectations to make sure that things are working better?

## Immersion Trip Thanks

Ty, chair of the immersion trips, sends a letter of thanks via e-mail to all the students who recently participated in the immersion trip to Mexico. Ty also copies the letter to the college president. He does so because he had a prior connection with the president through another organization. The president of the immersion trip organization and advisor are surprised by the e-mail and do not feel that Ty went through the "proper channels" before sending it. Although they appreciate the letter, they both agree that Ty should have run the e-mail through them first.

- What are the issues in this case?
- What are the president's options for handling the situation? How might each option play out? Which option do you prefer?
- Have you ever heard of the phrase "choose your battles"? Do you think this is a battle worth confronting? Should the president address the problem directly with Ty or should he make a general announcement to all the members of the group? What might happen if the president chooses not to address the situation?

# GENERAL LEADERSHIP CASES

## End-of-Year Inconvenience

Y ou are in charge of planning your organization's end-of-year picnic. Your school is on quarters, which makes determining a date for your event challenging. Although you try not to plan events close to the end of the quarter, your executive board members convince you that it's okay to plan this year's picnic to coincide with the last week of classes. They make this decision during the first week of the quarter, and everyone verbally commits to making the event a success.

The end-of-year picnic quickly approaches and members find themselves preparing for final exams. The picnic turns out to be a major event with a lot of details to be coordinated. Routinely members fail to follow through with their assignments. They hide behind finals but you know that many of them are burned out at the end of the year and are simply out of steam. You believe you still need to hold them accountable but struggle to find a balance between respecting their academic pressures and pulling off a good event. You are also concerned that if they don't step up and do their jobs you will be left coordinating the entire event, thus sacrificing your own studies.

- What are the issues in this case?
- What are your options for handling the situation? How might each option play out? Which option do you prefer?
- Is it fair that you do all the work? Should you cancel the event? Should you make members follow through with their commitments to the event?
- When are the best times to plan events on your campus? Is it better to host fewer events during key times or host more events during less

convenient times? How do you coordinate your events around other major events? Is scheduling a challenge on your campus? How do you work out the details?

## Slow Down

Elise is a student at Novell University. She holds a 3.5+ grade point average (GPA) and is very involved in campus life and enjoys the activities immensely. She is president of the student government, secretary of her sorority, peer mentor for a living learning program, and research assistant for her chemistry professor. This year happens to be especially busy for the campus groups because the university is undergoing a merger with a smaller institution and life on campus is changing with the merger.

During the fifth week of school, Elise is especially overcommitted; she has a huge lab report due for her chemistry research position, and her sorority is offering bids to prospective sisters. She promises the chemistry professor that she will have the report to him by 1:00 P.M. On her way to dropping it off before her calculus exam, she runs into some sorority sisters and they ask her for the minutes from the last two meetings, because they need to take them to the University Greek Council that evening. She tells them that she has not typed them up yet but promises that she will as soon as she completes her exam.

Elise takes her calculus exam and feels pretty good about how she did. On her way back to her hall, she stops by the student union for a bite to eat and runs into some of her residents. They give her a hard time about missing the last few programs in the hall. She tells them that she has been very busy and will try to make the next one. They remind her that there is one tomorrow evening and that it would be great if she could assist with the event. She tells them to count on her being there.

The next day in composition class, the professor is handing back papers and Elise gets quite upset when she finds that she got a C. She stays after class to talk with the professor. The professor tells her that late papers are graded down and since her paper was four days late that's why she got a lower grade. Elise is confused and says that she must have mixed up her dates. When she returns to her residence hall room she has five messages. All are from upset individuals. Her chemistry supervisor is upset because he didn't receive the lab report, the sorority president is upset about not having the minutes for the Greek Council meeting, and three of her residents are upset because she didn't follow through on other commitments. Elise doesn't understand how things have gotten so out of control.

- What are the issues in this case?
- What are Elise's options for handling the situation? How might each option play out? Which option do you prefer?
- What do you recommend that Elise do to get her life back under control? What offices on campus should Elise consult for help?

## Where Are the Minutes?

Sinead is the secretary of a student organization. Some of the executive board members are frustrated with her. Minutes are not going out on time, and when they do, they are inaccurate. To prompt her to do her job correctly, the president sends her a copy of the constitution with her responsibilities highlighted.

- What are the issues in this case?
- What are the options for handling the situation? How might each option play out? Which option do you prefer?
- What are your impressions of the president's attempt to rectify the situation? Do you believe the strategy is passive or active?
- If Sinead continues to neglect her responsibilities, what would you recommend be done next to motivate her? How many warnings should Sinead be given before she is removed from her position?

## "Stealing" from the Concession Box

Ryan is in charge of concession money at the end of basketball games at Port College. The position of concession team leader is unpaid but very prestigious for finance majors. It is so well regarded outside Port College by prospective employers that once students reach their junior and senior years, they compete heavily for the role. Ryan was selected his junior year, which means he will fill the role for two years.

One night Ryan is late getting to the main concession stand to count the money. It must be counted by two individuals before being put in the safe for the night, which can only be opened by the recreation center coordinator, Roxanne; they do not make nightly deposits at the bank. Ryan counts the money and signs off that the count is accurate. He places the money in the safe and heads out for the night.

The next night Ryan is running late again, and when he gets to the main concession stand, he finds that the women in charge are not very happy and really want to get going. They give him their total and then one of the women groans, "Come on, hurry up. We have places to be this evening." Ryan replies, "I *am* hurrying. I was at lab and it ran over. Why don't you just go ahead and I'll take care of this." The woman says, "Are you sure? We don't want to get into trouble." Ryan reassures her, "Don't worry, I trust you. And besides, how off could your count be?"

As Ryan begins counting the money, a couple of his fraternity brothers stop by to tell him about a party that they are going to. "Hurry up and you can make it. Meet us at the room in twenty minutes and then we can jump in my car," says his friend. Ryan replies, "I'll try, but if I'm not there, just go ahead without me." His friends leave and he continues counting the money and gets the same total as the women did.

Ryan is excited about the party. He is pretty sure Andrea will be there and he really wants to get to know her. She is in his sister sorority but the two have not had a chance to talk. As Ryan gets ready to leave, he remembers that he did not have a chance to get to the ATM and finds he has no cash. He thinks, "I could just borrow some from the concession stand, pay it back in the morning, and get the box in the safe before Roxanne knows it isn't there. Plus, tomorrow is Saturday and she won't be in until Monday." He takes forty dollars out of the box and hurries to his residence hall room to drop the box and get a quick shower. He makes his ride and has a blast at the party.

The next day, Ryan wakes up around noon and sees that he has three phone messages from Roxanne. When he finally calls her, she is very upset and tells him that she was just about to call the police to report the box missing. He tells her that he forgot to put it in the safe and will have it over in a flash. In the midst of worrying about the box, Ryan forgets that he borrowed the forty dollars and gives the box to Roxanne. When she does the count, she discovers the missing money and asks him who was working the stand last night. He tells her and she decides to fine the group the forty dollars. Ryan is sure that if he confesses his wrongdoing she will fire him, which will reduce his chances of getting a good job in the financial world.

- What are the issues in this case?
- What are Ryan's and Roxanne's options for handling the situation? How might each option play out? Which option do you prefer?
- Was it stealing when Ryan decided to borrow the money from the box? What are the ethical implications of Ryan's behavior if he is never caught?
- If the group finds out that Ryan took the money and never admitted it, what should they do? Should they seek punishment for Ryan? If so, what action should be taken?

## You Didn't Miss Me When I Was Gone?

Rachael is an active student leader during her first two and a half years of college. She is extremely involved in a student organization and is being groomed to be president. As a Spanish major, she is required to study abroad for one semester. She opts to study abroad during the second semester of her junior year, because two of her friends will be studying with her in Mexico. This is a difficult decision for Rachael, because second-semester juniors are typically elected president of her organization. This way they serve as president for one semester as a junior and one semester as a senior. Studying abroad during the second semester means that she will no longer be eligible to be president, but Rachael is satisfied with her decision and looks forward to her experience in Mexico.

Transitioning back to the United States for her senior year is challenging for Rachael, as it is for most students who study abroad. People are excited to see her but few have a sincere interest in hearing about her experiences in Mexico. Rachael is amazed that life in the States seems to have moved on without her. She is eager to pick up where she left off and hopes that she will find comfort in the organization that meant so much to her.

During Rachael's semester away, Shandra, the new president of the organization, started some new initiatives and also recruited many new members.

There are new officers, new programs, and new goals for the organization. Although Shandra warmly welcomes Rachael back during the first meeting of the organization, Rachael now feels very awkward in the organization that she helped build. She doesn't know if she will want to continue to be involved in the organization.

- What are the issues in this case for Rachael? For Shandra?
- What are Rachael's and Shandra's options for handling the situation? How might each option play out? Which option do you prefer?
- Should Shandra want Rachael's active participation? Why might she be hesitant to involve Rachael in the group?
- Is Rachael still an asset to the organization? Whose responsibility is it to involve Rachael in the organization? Do you have any recommendations for how she might get reconnected with the group?
- How might student organization leaders welcome back students who have been studying abroad in a way that makes them feel appreciated?

## One Leader Does Not an Organization Make

Christian is very committed to his student organization. Because the organization membership is small, he not only serves as president but also is in charge of public relations. Despite Christian's appointed positions, he tends to "take over" the responsibilities of other officers in the group. Many of the members think he is a control freak. He plans the programs, advertises them, coordinates all the details, and then takes all the credit. Because he is the one coordinating most of the events, he is also typically the only person in the organization who knows the details. The members feel left out and believe that Christian just wants to make the rest of them look bad. Christian believes that he is doing what is best for the organization. In the past, a few of the members did not follow through with their commitments, and he just wants to make sure that things get done correctly. In his opinion, he is helping the others. They should be grateful that he's willing to shoulder most of the responsibility for their events. This frees up the other members to focus on their studies. What Christian doesn't realize is that the real reason he takes over is that he is insecure about his leadership and doing it all allows him to prove himself to the group.

- What are the issues in this case for Christian? What are the issues for the other members of the organization?
- What are the options for handling the situation? How might each option play out? Which option do you prefer?
- Have you ever been part of an organization where you felt someone was doing all the work and taking all the credit? If so, how did you handle the situation? Did you quit? Why do you think some people quit instead of working on resolving the situation?
- Have you ever felt that you were doing all the work for your organization? If so, why did you do all the work? Why didn't you talk with the other members? Do you think you were perceived by your members in the same way that Christian was perceived by his?
- Why is communication so important within an organization? Why is it detrimental to an organization if only one person knows what is going on? What is the preferred mode of communication for your organization? Is it effective?

## Men/Women in Charge

The leadership of your organization is predominantly male. The group elected the officers, and the men appear to be in charge of everything. During general meetings, they speak first, tend to influence the group, and dominate the meetings. The women in the organization believe that the group lacks inclusiveness. They do not want to quit, but they do not appreciate the male-dominated culture of the organization. Two female members bring this problem to the attention of the president, but he dismisses their concerns by reminding them that they elected the officers. The women are frustrated. Elections for new officers are a year away and they feel trapped in this gender-imbalanced organization.

- What are the issues in this case?
- What are the options for handling the situation? How might each option play out? Which option do you prefer?
- What should the women do if they try to address the gender dynamics with the entire group but again are dismissed?

- Have you ever been part of a group where you felt your voice was not heard? Are your organizations inclusive of men and women? Are they inclusive of students of color?
- What do you think draws people to your organization? What keeps them? How diverse is your organization? How intentional are you about making sure that all members feel included and valued?

## Upholding the Organization's Constitution

The constitution of your organization states that members will be held accountable for their actions. It is expected that all executive board members attend all major events. Lorraine, a member of the executive board, fails to attend an important event for your organization. She did not inform any member of the organization that she would be absent. When Amber, the president, approaches Lorraine about why she didn't attend the event, Lorraine admits that she forgot about it. Referencing the constitution, Amber informs her that she cannot participate in the group's next event. This decision causes a huge conflict within the organization; some of the members favor the decision and others oppose it. No one has ever been asked to "sit out" an event. The members believe that this is a scare tactic to get Lorraine, and any others who are not active contributing members, to quit the organization. Lorraine does exactly that. Those who oppose Amber's decision are left wondering who is the next to go.

- What are the issues in this case?
- What are the options for handling the situation? How might each option play out? Which option do you prefer?
- If Lorraine played a major role in the coordination of the event and then failed to show up, would you be in favor of Amber's decision? If this wasn't Lorraine's first time missing an event, would Amber's decision be justified? Should Amber have consulted with the executive board before making her decision?
- How do you currently hold members of your organization responsible for their actions? How do you communicate your expectations for the general members of your group? The executive board? Should there

be set consequences for not following through with commitments made to the organization?

# Ego Test

Danita, a sophomore, is the new president of your organization. She was elected president because she is organized, enthusiastic, and extremely committed to the organization's success. She ran unopposed but the membership in general seems happy with its new leader. As the semester progresses and Danita becomes familiar with her role, she becomes more and more effective. She motivates the group, holds members accountable, and gives lots of praise.

A junior member of the organization, Wanda, volunteers to hang posters for an upcoming event. However, she doesn't get the posters hung until the night before the event. As a result, very few people are aware of the event and attendance is low. Danita confronts Wanda about her lateness in hanging the posters and Wanda gets very upset and offensive. She tells Danita that she is an ineffective leader, and that since she's only a sophomore she shouldn't be telling her what to do. Wanda reminds Danita that she's been in the organization longer than Danita has and that she knows what is best for the group.

- What are the issues in this case?
- What are Danita's options for handling the situation? How might each option play out? Which option do you prefer?
- Do you think Danita would react the same way if she were a senior? Should Danita's age be a factor?
- Have you had experiences when younger students have had to instruct or lead older students? If so, how did the older students handle the situation? Is it harder to have someone who is younger than you tell you what to do?
- Do you ever question someone's leadership ability because of his or her age? Do you ever assume that because someone is a senior he or she will make the best leader for the organization or that younger members should have less responsibility?

## Charge It!

Your organization sponsors a speaker on campus. Although you receive money from the student activity fund to pay for the event, your president asks you to purchase the submarines, chips, drinks, and cookies for the social that will take place after the event. He tells you that you cannot spend more than $300 on food and that the university will reimburse you. Being the diligent student organization member that you are, you charge $300 worth of food on your private credit card. You promptly file the necessary paperwork to be reimbursed. Almost two months after you filed the request, you still have not received your money. Your credit card company is charging you interest on the unpaid amount. You ask the president how long you will have to wait for the reimbursement, and he tells you that the university reimbursement system is very slow. It could take another month. Frustrated, you wish he had told you this in the beginning, because then you wouldn't have used your personal credit card to purchase the food.

- What are the issues in this case?
- What are your options for handling the situation? How might each option play out? Which option do you prefer?
- Do you think that if you had spent more than the allocated $300 you should be reimbursed the additional money?
- What could you do to expedite the reimbursement process? Who could assist you?
- Have you ever been asked to purchase something for your organization with your own money? How does your organization handle reimbursement? Is there any protocol for how to pay for organization-related items?
- Does your organization have a credit card? If so, what are your protocols for using the credit card?

## Homecoming Violation

Manuel is the chair of this year's homecoming parade. Before Manuel assumes the position, last year's chair, Stella, informs him of an incident with the local brewery that took place at last year's event. Although the parade rules strictly prohibit the consumption and promotion of alcohol at the parade, the local brewery violated both rules. People on the float were consuming alcohol and wearing T-shirts that promoted drinking. As a result, the group was not invited to participate in this year's parade. The owner of the establishment calls Manuel to get information about this year's parade. Manuel reminds him of the situation that took place last year and the owner gets very upset. He argues that there was no alcohol on the float and calls the students liars.

- What are the issues in this case?
- What are Manuel's options for handling the situation? How might each option play out? Which option do you prefer?
- If Manuel does not let the brewery participate in the parade, what are the potential consequences? If Manuel does let the brewery participate, what are the potential consequences? If the university is trying to improve community relations, how might Manuel's decision factor into this goal? How do you define community relations?
- Have you ever been in a situation in which you had to deliver someone else's bad news? If so, how did you handle it? Does the fact that the information Manuel is giving the brewery owner is based on information he's received from the past chair make it more difficult for Manuel to defend? If so, how?
- Is it sometimes difficult to deliver unpopular news to an adult? How do you handle a difficult conversation, especially if the person gets angry?

## The Perils of Co-Chairs

This year your organization elects two chairs, or co-chairs, instead of one. As co-chairs, Jackson and Mikaela will work together, sharing the responsibility and time commitment. Prior to assuming their position, the two are good friends and have worked together planning two events for the organization. About two months into their shared chairpersonship, it becomes clear that Jackson isn't following through with his responsibilities. He comes to meetings late and unprepared. The day of a major event for the organization, he text-messages Mikaela asking her both the location and time of the event. Mikaela is furious. This is the last straw. She wants to confront Jackson and tell him that he needs to do a better job or else she will address the problem with the rest of the organization, but she is afraid that he will quit the organization altogether. She also worries that she will lose his friendship.

- What are the issues in this case?
- What are Mikaela's options for handling the situation? How might each option play out? Which option do you prefer?
- Why do you think Mikaela is hesitant to confront Jackson? Have you ever been in a situation in which you were frustrated with a member and were more likely to ignore the behavior rather than confront the situation? If so, why did you react that way?
- If Jackson is confronted, do you think he will quit the organization? Should that be Mikaela's goal? Have you ever been confronted about something and become hostile? If so, why did you behave that way? How could the situation have been handled better?

## Pick a Side

This year's presidential election is very close. José was the previous president, but he loses the reelection to Rick, a newer member of the organization. José is clearly upset by the outcome of the election but wants to remain in the organization, so he grudgingly assumes the role of the group's parliamentarian. The executive board is quickly divided into two groups. Half support Rick, the new president, and are willing to give him a chance. The others clearly support José and are determined to get Rick to resign. José's supporters make meetings difficult by disagreeing with Rick and limiting the progress toward his goals. Some have even gone so far as to purposefully not follow through on assigned tasks so that events will fail, thus making Rick look bad. Rick is aware of these overt attacks and has stepped in on several occasions to pick up the slack and save organization events. He does this because he believes that he needs to prove himself as a team player and that eventually he will win over the entire group.

- What are the issues in this case?
- What are Rick's options for handling the situation? How might each option play out? Which option do you prefer?
- What do you suggest that Rick do to lead the organization? What do you think of his "work hard and win them over" approach?
- What help, if any, could the organization's advisor provide?
- Have you ever been part of an organization in which you wished one person had been elected to an office over another? If so, how did you treat this person? How did the other members of your organization treat this person? Is it fair to purposefully make things difficult on an officer you don't prefer?
- How would you feel if you were in Rick's position? How would you feel if you were in José's position? Would you encourage the deviant behavior in the hopes that if Rick resigned you could be president?

## Academic Sacrifice

Li is an extremely active student leader. He is president of his fraternity as well as senior orientation leader, he facilitates freshmen leadership training sessions, he is the captain of his intramural basketball team, and he regularly volunteers at the local food pantry. As a tribute to his involvement and outstanding leadership abilities, Li was even elected homecoming king for his college. Even with the demands of all of his activities, Li is also an honors student.

One of the graduation requirements for all honors students is that they complete an honors thesis. This thesis is based on original research that is evaluated by a faculty member. Final theses are due the semester before a student graduates. In Li's case, his thesis is due in December for a May graduation. Because Li is so involved in student organizations, he asks his advisor for a two-month extension on his honors thesis. His advisor hesitates to grant his request but then decides to make the necessary arrangements so that Li can complete his thesis in February. Li lets his organizational commitments take precedence over his academic deadlines, and February comes and goes and Li still hasn't completed his thesis. Li meets with his advisor, who informs him that despite his high GPA and completion of all the honors courses, without his thesis, he cannot graduate with honors.

- What are the issues in this case?
- What are Li's options for handling the situation? How might each option play out? Which option do you prefer? What were Li's options prior to February?
- What do you think of Li's decision to focus on fulfilling his student leadership responsibilities rather than on completing his thesis?
- Do you know students who put their involvement ahead of their academics? Do you ever put your involvement ahead of your academics? How do you prioritize your commitments?

## Office Space

Office space for student organizations is very limited on your campus. Each year, for the more than fifty organizations that request offices, only fifteen offices are randomly assigned. Luckily, your organization is allocated one of these highly sought offices this year. To keep your assigned space, your organization is required to post and maintain at least thirty office hours per week. To meet this requirement, your executive board decides that each officer will keep five office hours per week. The first two weeks of the semester the officers are good about maintaining their hours. As the semester progresses, however, they start skipping hours. When you, the president of the organization, address the issue with the executive board, the officers reveal that they think the policy is ridiculous and a waste of their time.

- What are the issues in this case?
- What are your options for handling the situation? How might each option play out? Which option do you prefer?
- What are the pros and cons of having office space?
- Have you ever had trouble motivating members of your organization to do something that they didn't want to do? If so, how did you handle the situation?

## Taking a Chance

As the organization's president, you have a vacancy on your executive board. You decide to take a chance and appoint Chloe, a rather inexperienced yet dedicated general board member. Chloe is a second-semester freshman and shows a great deal of potential. She eagerly accepts the position. As the president, you offer to help her learn her role and invite her to ask you any questions. Because Chloe wishes to prove her worth to the organization on her own, she doesn't ask you for any help. Within a month of accepting the position, Chloe finds herself completely overwhelmed. She isn't sure what to do and is surprised that there is no training manual or previous information detailing her role and responsibilities. She is afraid to tell you that she is so unsure of herself, because she is worried that you will think she is dumb or incompetent. She decides to quit the organization instead and tells you that it's just too much to manage along with her schoolwork.

- What are the issues in this case?
- What are your options for handling the situation? How might each option play out? Which option do you prefer?
- Are Chloe's feelings justified? Can you understand why she might feel overwhelmed and not be willing to admit it?
- How does your organization train its new officers? Is there a training manual for new officers? Do you spend time orienting them or do you just assume that they will "figure things out"? How can organization leaders be more intentional about training new officers?

## Got Your Insurance Card?

Your executive board attends your regional conference in a neighboring state. One of your members, Katoria, gets very sick. She's having trouble breathing and has to be taken to the hospital. Upon arrival, you learn that she doesn't have her insurance card. She thinks it is somewhere in her residence hall room. She informs you that her parents are out of town and cannot be reached.

- What are the issues in this case?
- What are your options for handling the situation? How might each option play out? Which option do you prefer?

- Who should be informed of her illness?
- How might you prevent a situation like this from happening in the future?

# Who's in Charge?

You advisor is somewhat disconnected from your organization. She attends some meetings and signs the necessary paperwork, but overall she provides little support to the organization. As the chapter president, you decide to ask her to be more involved in the organization. It looks like she took your feedback well, because she starts to get more involved in the organization. As she gets to know the members better, she starts pulling them aside and telling them who isn't doing his or her job. Her "sidebar" conversations are divisive and inappropriate. You learn that a great deal of her criticism centers around your leadership ability.

- What are the issues in this case?
- What are your options for handling the situation? How might each option play out? Which option do you prefer?
- What is the role of your advisor? Do you and your advisor talk about your clear expectations for one another? Given that your advisor is a volunteer, how much time do you think he or she should have to spend fulfilling that role?

# Soccer Tournament Debacle

Craig is a co-captain of the men's soccer team at Salty University on the East Coast. He was a star player for his first three years and always wanted to be captain. When he was selected at the end of his junior year, he was elated. He was also excited because the team elected Pete, his teammate for the last three years and also his housemate. Both team members are true leaders on the soccer field, winning numerous recognitions and awards for their achievements. In addition, both like to party with teammates and colleagues from other sports. The varsity soccer coach has a strict drinking policy during the season: simply put, no drinking allowed. At Salty U., soccer is a fall sport, so the season begins a few weeks before the semester in August and ends sometime around November, depending on how far the team advances during postseason play.

The soccer team at Salty U. is known for its wild parties but manages to stay out of trouble with the university and the town. A number of the men took up residence in a house, so it was dubbed the "soccer house." For all intents and purposes, it operates much like a fraternity house. The house throws parties and hosts prospective soccer recruits during campus visits.

In October, the team is invited to participate in a collegiate soccer tournament. Salty U. does not have the budget to send the entire team, so just the travel team makes the trip. In all, eighteen men—the players, the head coach, an assistant, and an athletic trainer—travel to the tournament. The team plays all its games and does quite well, taking second place out of twelve teams. The coach is very proud of the men and takes them out to dinner to celebrate. He tells them that those players over twenty-one can have one drink with dinner, but no more. After dinner they need to go back to their rooms and get to bed early so they can leave for the airport by 6 A.M.

The team members return to their hotel after dinner, and a few of them meet in Craig and Pete's room to hang out. Craig says, "Let's go check out the sights." Pete adds, "Coach will never find out. Besides, we are done, so what would he do?" Eight members decide that they will go check out the town.

At 6:00 the next morning, as the team members are loading up their vehicle to head to the airport, Coach notices that four of the members are missing and that one of them is Pete. He asks Craig to go and check his room again to see if Pete is still there. Craig does so, and when he returns, he tells Coach that Pete isn't there. Craig knows that Pete and three others never returned last night, but he keeps that to himself. He looks at the others who went out last night but isn't sure what he can do to help his missing teammates. Just then, a taxi pulls up and out jump Pete and the others. They still have to pack up their belongings in their rooms.

The trip to the airport begins with a speech from Coach. He reminds the players of the rules and that they are still within the season. "Just because we were out of the tournament did not give you the right to violate training rules. I want some answers. Pete, you are a team captain and you are supposed to be setting an example for the rest of the team. I want to know who was involved or you all are going to be suspended for the next game." The next game is against their conference archrivals, and they have a good shot at beating them and winning the conference title.

At the airport, the players huddle together and discuss the situation. The players who did not go out feel that the eight who did owe it to them to come clean and face their punishment. Craig says, "Are you kidding me? We would lose with all of us being suspended. I think Pete and you three should say it was just you and give us a shot at the conference title."

- What are the issues in this case?
- What are the options for handling the situation? How might each option play out? Which option do you prefer?
- Do you think Pete and Craig should both come clean? Do you think they owe it to their teammates as leaders? Should some be suspended and not others? How do you decide who gets suspended?
- Should the importance of the next game be considered?

## You Aren't Any Fun Anymore

As president of your organization, you are the one ultimately responsible for the behavior of the group. You stay sober at social functions so that you can determine if intoxicated and out-of-control members need to be disciplined. You are trying to please the group but have to hold members accountable. It is very difficult to discipline friends. Your friends in the club start to criticize you for not being "fun" anymore. You know that what you are doing is right but you also miss partying with your friends.

- What are the issues in this case?
- What are your options for handling the situation? How might each option play out? Which option do you prefer?
- As president, is there anyone outside your organization who can offer you support?
- Why is it important as the president to remain sober at functions? Are you really responsible for your members?

# 12

# ADVICE FOR
# STUDENT LEADERS

We felt that the best way to conclude this book would be to provide some helpful tips, so we asked current student leaders for their advice for newer organization officers. Their words of wisdom follow. Rather than organize the organizational leaders' suggestions around themes or categories, we felt they should be listed the same way they were given—randomly. We believe these recommendations are important and did not prioritize one idea over another. The reader may review and discuss the advice starting at the beginning, the end, or any point in between.

- Don't get overcommitted; you need time with your friends.
- Build up your leadership involvement slowly. Don't sign up for everything in your first semester. Overdoing it may lead to low grades during your first semester.
- Set clear boundaries and know your limits.
- Remember that you can be an advocate for students even if you are not a member of their group.
- Remember that strategic planning and goal setting are important to planning.
- Plan with sensitivity. Keep in mind stress points of the academic year.
- Don't underestimate that even the simplest tasks can be a major time commitment (e.g., e-mailing every organization on campus). Ask what is involved before agreeing to do something.
- Remember that it is okay to make mistakes; just admit them.
- Figure out who can be counted on and who cannot. Some advisors and administrators are more helpful than others.

- Reply to e-mail as soon as possible. Otherwise, you might get way behind and miss something important.
- Be involved in a variety of organizations. This way you will get to know a lot of different people.
- Ask questions. You won't be annoying anyone. In fact, people will be more annoyed if you don't ask and you do something wrong.
- Think about how you present yourself. When you are a student leader, people look up to you. Don't be loud and obnoxious.
- Have fun.
- Be available.
- Establish your leadership style and tell your members what they can expect from you.
- Keep a rainy-day fund so you'll always have money for your organization.
- Remember that communication is key. Don't be afraid to use the phone or walk into someone's office to talk with that person. E-mail can only do so much.
- Get to know your advisor.
- Network with students, administrators, and community members.
- Get involved in fund-raising.
- Be supportive of other organizations' causes and programs.
- Work with other student groups. Collaboration is important.
- Enjoy being a swimmer (general member) for a while before becoming a lifeguard (leader). Make sure you have ample time to enjoy being a new/general member.
- Be responsible and accountable but don't take your role as a leader too seriously. Enjoy the experience.
- Have good friends outside of your organization.
  Remember that your leadership positions and the skills that you learn as a student leader will shape your life. Be sure you maximize your opportunities.
- Be flexible, because it is very hard to predict what will happen in planning an event.
- Be as prepared as possible and be ready to troubleshoot.
- If you want to assume a leadership position for your organization, first shadow the person currently in the position to get a good sense of what the position entails. This will also help with transition.

- Don't ever assume that something will get done.
- Make sure that several members of your organization, if not all, know what's going on.
- Make sure that you know within your organization who can make decisions on behalf of the group and who cannot. Don't make decisions without the appropriate permission.
- Stay calm.
- Lead by example. Never ask anyone to do anything that you aren't willing to do yourself.
- Learn from your mistakes. No one is perfect.
- Remember that it's okay to say no to cosponsors. Cosponsorship needs to mean more than simply giving your organization money and putting your name on the event.
- Keep general members involved. This will impact retention.
- Make your meetings efficient but fun so that members will keep attending.
- Start meetings on time.
- Remember that you are in school to be a student first.
- Remember that time management is key. Keep a calendar, a to-do list, and a list of priorities.
- Be yourself—people can tell when you are disingenuous.
- Leave a legacy through delegation. If you see someone who has potential, give that person a job.
- Remember that it is okay to fail in order to learn a larger lesson.
- Build relationships with administration and encourage others to build them as well.
- Treat people with respect.
- Don't lose yourself in your organizations.
- Allow everyone the opportunity to contribute to the agenda and then prioritize the agenda.
- Invest in coalition building. Share resources, people, and power.
- Show your appreciation for others and reward hard work.
- Remember that leadership is about empowering others. Be inclusive and give others opportunities.
- Remember that elections are not about the competition. Find ways to get everyone who is interested involved.

- Recognize that as a leader you will have victories and defeats. Some people will like you and some people won't. Don't take it personally.
- Don't let others' opinions of you cause self-doubt.
- Keep your ego in check. You are not a leader for yourself; you are working for a greater purpose.
- Take time to reflect on your successes and learn from your defeats.
- Be reliable. Be at meetings on time and be prepared.
- Meet one-on-one with key constituents to learn their opinions and gather their feedback.
- Try not to take the job home with you; you need a break.
- Recognize that you will only get out of your organization what you put into it.
- Use many hands to make the workload light.
- Remember that food and free T-shirts are helpful in increasing participation.
- Recognize that although consensus decision making helps people feel that they are part of the group, this type of decision making is not always possible.
- Recognize that although it is important to challenge the status quo, you need to work within the system and know your limits.
- Don't overprogram at the end of the year. People are tired and they won't be as committed because of finals. Make end-of-year programs manageable, or else you'll be planning them yourself.
- Have clear expectations for your members.
- Don't mix up your priorities. You need to do well in your classes; a minimum GPA for a group is a good thing.
- Make sure that your organization's goals and priorities align with your school's priorities.
- Understand the political landscape of your university. Just because you feel supported doesn't mean that you are supported.
- Be a good role model.
- Keep your eye on the big picture and don't get bogged down in all the little details.
- Make friends with someone you can vent to and trust.
- Set goals at the beginning of the school year. Your organization needs direction.
- Do things because you care.

- Avoid dating within your organization.
- Be respectful of individuality; everyone is different.
- Get enough sleep.
- Attend class.
- Be open to your own professional growth.